The Wish for Power
and the Fear
of Having It

The Wish for Power and the Fear of Having It

Althea J. Horner, M.D.

Jason Aronson Inc., Northvale, New Jersey, London

The publisher gratefully acknowledges permission from International Creative Management, Inc. to quote from Arthur Miller's "I Don't Need You Anymore," originally published in *Esquire* magazine.

Library of Congress Cataloging-in-Publication Data

Horner, Althea J.
  The wish for power and the fear of having it.

  Bibliography: p.
  Includes index.
  1. Interpersonal relations.   2. Power (Social
sciences)   3. Control (Psychology)   I. Title.
HM132.H67 1989   303.3   88-3328
ISBN 0-87668-924-1

Manufactured in the United States of America

Jason Aronson Inc. offers books and cassettes. For information and catalog write to:
Jason Aronson Inc., 230 Livingston Street, Northvale, NJ 07647.

To Douglas, Stuart, Andrew, Daniel, and Robert

The child is father to the man—William Wordsworth

Contents

Contents

Preface

I was moved to write this book because I believe that the role of power in human motivation and behavior is seriously unappreciated and underestimated. Nietzsche concluded that the will to power was *the* primary motivational force. He believed that although people claimed that what they wanted most in life was happiness, in reality what they wanted most was power. He thought that they could not acknowledge this since it would be immoral and contrary to other values. He firmly believed that happiness, pleasure, and exaltation come from feeling powerful. Anyone who watches television productions such as "The Wild Kingdom" is familiar with scenes of bucks crashing antler to antler as they fight for dominance over females of the herd for first choice of mate, or with scenes of animals demarking their territory by spraying urine around its perimeter. One does not have to look far to see parallels in human behavior. Rival gangs fight mini-wars over "turf" in our inner cities. Denied the subtler, more "civilized" forms of power within the larger society, the struggle for raw power, untamed by civilization, comes to the fore. Meanwhile, the local high school football hero claims the Prom Queen as his date for the big dance.

Although we need not accept Nietzsche's views as definitive of the human species, we would do well to keep in mind his observation that the wish for power does pervade all aspects of human behavior. Power issues need to be identified, made explicit, and understood in terms of how power is used to compensate for and defend against the anxiety and shame of powerlessness. With this knowledge, power as an issue per se can be separated out from whatever else is going on in a relationship or situation. To paraphrase an old adage: when power comes in the window, love goes out the door! With a predominant need for power, there is no room for tenderness, nurturance, affection, play, or any other facet of intimacy.

Power as a motivating force will also inevitably contaminate the creative process as well as the ability to construct and move toward healthy and gratifying life goals.

The Wish for Power and the Fear of Having It will endeavor to provide the reader with insights into the kinds of power issues that may be standing in the way of his or her ability to achieve life goals both in the arena of personal relationships and in that of work and career. Instead of being held hostage either to the need for power, or to a fear of having it, people can come to see power as an inner resource, a constructive force in their lives.

In *Being and Loving* I wrote about the developmental process that leads to the establishment of a secure sense of one's own identity and the capacity for intimacy. The book focused on the nature of the conflict between *being* (identity) and *loving* (intimacy), and how people attempt to deal with that conflict.

Central to the development of every human being is the laying down, in the first three years of life, of a basic image and structure of the self, along with a basic sense of others and of the self in relation to those others. The body of psychoanalytic theory that addresses this aspect of development is called object relations theory. The fundamental image of the self is referred to as the "self representation," while the fundamental image of the other is called the "object representation." These mental structures, that endure over time, although they do become more complex, come about as the result of a combination of three factors: (1) the quality of the relationship with the primary caretaker (usually the mother); (2) the child's innate and constitutional physical and temperamental tendencies; and (3) the way in which the child experiences, and ultimately conceptualizes, his or her unique world. These inner schemata of the self and the other, and the nature of their interrelationship in the mind, contribute significantly to the manner in which the self and others are experienced in interpersonal relationships throughout the rest of one's life. They particularly contribute to the conflict expressed by so many, between "being me" and "loving you."

This book will follow the same developmental path, but from a different perspective—that of the power dimension. Each stage of object relations development is characterized by a particular balance of power between the child and the primary mothering person, and subsequently the father as well. In later years, the individual's experience of power versus powerlessness and of the associated pride versus shame will bear the stamp of the early years of development and will be played out in adult interpersonal relationships.

In the following chapters I explore our relationship to power from a psychological and developmental point of view, looking at the various ramifications of its historical unfolding within the individual in the context of his or her family of origin. Because all babies share certain commonalities of caretaking experience as well as of physical and neurological unfolding, even allowing for a wide range of personal and cultural differences within their families, certain universal themes emerge. Each stage of the earliest years of psychological development has its own power correlates, and from each of these stages are derived later power issues for the individual.

Hopefully, this book will enable its readers to confront their conflicts with respect to their own power and to that of others, and will empower them to resolve these conflicts in a manner that enhances their feelings toward themselves and improve the quality of their interpersonal relationships in both the world of work and the world of love.

Althea J. Horner
Los Angeles, California

Part I

The Range of Power

1

The Power Dimension

The American fascination with the power of great wealth is seen in the success of the television series "Dallas," "Falcon Crest," and "Dynasty." J.R. Ewing, Angela Channing, and Blake Carrington are the epitome of power through wealth. Everyone loves to hate J.R. Ewing. Yet, there is an involvement, a fascination, and perhaps a wished-for identification with these characters. The writers and producers wisely give them enough positive human characteristics to allow the viewer to identify with their power, or to allow the fantasy of being in their benevolent control. J.R. is a loving and devoted father to his son and son to his mother. Angela Channing fights for her children like a tigress when they are threatened by outside forces, although she may just as easily turn her power against them. J.R., on the other hand, would never turn against his son, which makes him a more positive figure than Angela. The only person Angela is consistently good to is the Chinese manservant, because he never challenges or endangers her power.

Surveying a group of men and women, I asked them what the term *power* meant to them. Some seemed most concerned with the issue of power in regard to relationships. Dennis A. wondered, "Is power always an issue in a relationship?" Sylvia J. spoke of the power of love, of "the things you will do for someone you love." But, she added, "Love can be used to manipulate the other." Edward Bulwer Lytton cynically echoed this observation

4

saying, "What's affection, but the power we give to another to torment us?"[1]

Others were concerned with what happens to them in relation to what is referred to as "formal power." Larry D. asked, "How can I maintain a sense of power when dealing with someone who, in fact, is in a position of power in relation to me?" His question brought to mind what a survivor of Auschwitz told a television reporter. "They may have been able to enslave my body, but they could never enslave my mind." Although situations with teachers or supervisors are not as malevolent as those in the concentration camp, the underlying principle is the same.

Still others I interviewed spoke of power in terms of effectiveness in the world: "Power is the ability to make things happen, to achieve results." Some linked this kind of power with money. "Money gives you power because you are free to do what you want." Others said, "Making decisions is power," or, "Competence and doing things well equal power." A woman named Barbara linked that kind of power with self-confidence, and saw self-confidence as coming from knowledge and understanding. Bill N., a professional man, noted that a brilliant mind is powerless if the person does not have the ability to communicate his or her ideas to others. Barbara put it somewhat differently: "Command of language and words gives you power in many situations because it is easier to get what you want from people or institutions." When one refers to "the power of the press," there is an acknowledgment of the power of words and ideas.

Some focused on the issue of powerlessness, in terms of people like the elderly or the poor, because of their inability to change their situations. This is clearly the antithesis of being able to make things happen.

Others were concerned with the abuse of power, in particular by people who have to make up for some deficiency felt to exist within themselves. Fred T. thought that everyone needs

---

[1]Edward Bulwer Lytton (1805–1873) *Darnley,* Act II, Scene 1.

some person or group that can be looked down on, because this gives them *feelings* of power if not actual power. Carried to its ultimate, of course, is the use of brute strength against another person. Some spoke of male dominance at home and in the workplace, white supremacy epitomized by apartheid, or situations in which big companies gobble up little companies in order to control a particular market.

A young businessman, Robert K., commented on emotional independence as power, saying that "power is the ability to control your own state of emotional well-being." So for him, power is an inner state that is independent of outside forces. He was speaking in terms of the desired outcome of healthy development contrasting with the illusory power that comes from a denial of one's need for others, a denial that serves to protect the individual from felt dangers of human relationships. In healthy development, the emotional nurturance provided by parents becomes "internalized" and is then part of one's *inner* resources. It is an aspect of what I will later describe as "intrinsic power."

George J. also used the word *control,* but in a very different way. He said, "I put power and control together. Power has the upper hand. In a relationship, the one with power is the one with the least amount at stake." According to the words of a popular song, "Freedom is another word for nothing left to lose." For George, power is another word for nothing left to lose. A defensive denial of caring, a refusal to let anyone really matter, may serve to protect the illusory power of a basically threatened self.

Through all of the interviews it was noted, either directly or indirectly, that power per se is neither good nor bad, and that its morality depends on how it is used. But even there we may run into questions such as "Does the end justify the means?" This most difficult of ethical dilemmas has been debated by philosophers throughout human history. Kant[2] went so far as to argue

---

[2]Immanuel Kant, *Groundwork of the Metaphysic of Morals* (1785).

that it is wrong to tell a lie even to save another man's life. He claimed that moral rules admit of no exceptions. Today the same question is answered in widely differing ways by government at all levels, and especially from nation to nation.

The wish for power may be second only to the need for love, and the two often go together. In some cases, the need for power is primary. In its benevolent form, power affords us leadership, protection, and security. In its malevolent form it brings domination or abuse. The power differential characterizing the relationship between a parent and a small child is the first and most formative experience with this inescapable dimension of life and of all subsequent interpersonal relationships. Our attitude toward that early experience will determine how we use our own later power (or how we refuse to use it), and how we react to the power of others—whether we seek it and cling to it, whether we hate and envy it, or whether we rebel against it, overtly or covertly.

The main thesis of Alfred Adler (1930), one of the pioneers of psychoanalysis who broke away from Freud, was that everyone struggles against a felt inferiority and attempts to become superior instead. "To be a human being means the possession of a feeling of inferiority that is constantly pressing towards its own conquest." The lowered self-esteem may come from some actual physical defect, but it may also come about in normal, healthy development because even the normal child feels small, helpless, and at the mercy of adults in the world in which it lives. A felt physical inferiority, such as short stature, may evoke a need to make oneself "big," an attitude that is characterized by some as "little man's disease." Napoleon is believed to have suffered in this way.

Adler said that in every individual there is a craving for power, for victory over the difficulties of life and that each child develops a strategy, a "life-style," aimed at elevating his or her self-esteem and the achievement of superiority. These goals will be manifest in useful ideals and achievement as well as in the domination of others. We can see this concept of powerlessness versus power, of shame versus pride embedded in Adler's ideas.

The link between power and pride is evident all about us. When an Iraqui plane damaged the USS *Stark* and killed several of its crew, the attack was referred to in the newspapers as a "humiliation." The press characteristically takes this attitude in its commentary on political and world events. A reporter wondered "Who blinked first?" when asking about an exchange between the president of the United States and the secretary general of the USSR. Issues of war and peace are often described in terms more appropriate to the adolescent game of "chicken." The dread of "losing face" is not the concern of Oriental nations alone.

Jay Haley (1969) tells us that "Power tactics are those maneuvers a person uses to give himself influence and control over his social world and so make that world more predictable. Defined thus broadly, a man has power if he can order someone to behave in a certain way, but he also has power if he can provoke someone to behave in that way." Sometimes it is not always obvious where the power really lies in a situation or relationship. Haley also observes that "Many individuals appear to consider the gain of power positions more important than any subjective distress they might experience" (p.6). The motivational importance of power in every facet of life is not to be underestimated!

The negative side of power has been emphasized by those who agree with English historian John Emerich Dalberg's words, "Power tends to corrupt; absolute power corrupts absolutely."[3] Percy Bysshe Shelley noted that

> *Power, like a desolating pestilence,*
> *Pollutes whate'er it touches; and obedience,*
> *Bane of all genius, virtue, freedom, truth,*
> *Makes slaves of men, and, of the human frame,*
> *A mechanized automaton.*[4]

---

[3]In a letter to Bishop Mandell Creighton (1887).
[4]Percy Bysshe Shelley, *Queen Mab III.*

And in *The Education of Henry Adams,* the author writes:

> Power is poison. Its effects on Presidents had always been
> tragic, chiefly as an almost insane excitement at first, and a
> worse reaction afterwards; but also because no mind is so
> well balanced as to bear the strain of seizing unlimited force
> without habit or knowledge of it; and finding it disputed with
> him by hungry packs of wolves and hounds whose lives de-
> pend on snatching the carrion.

Spinoza[5] warned that when passion for fame, power, and
money takes over the person's reason for being, and when these
needs become ends in themselves, this passion becomes a form of
insanity.

Further considering the effect on the holder of power, Tillotson[6] reflected that

> Those who are in highest places, and have the most power,
> have the least liberty, because they are the most observed.

We might add that, because they are the most envied they are
certain to be confronted by challenges to their power.

This book delves into the evolution of power in the self, how
it is manifested in interpersonal interaction, and how expressed in
the world at large. It will compare different kinds of power—that
which is intrinsic to the individual, that which is real and that
which is illusory, as well as defensive and compensatory power.
How do we live with power, our own and that of others? What
marks the difference between the constructive and destructive use
of power—the difference between a Gandhi or a Hitler?

The continuum of power—at one end residing within the self
and, at the other, residing in power over others in both the interpersonal and political spheres—opens the question as to the relation-

---

[5]Benedict de Spinoza, *Ethics* (1672).
[6]John Tillotson, *Reflections* (1630–1694).

ship between these extremes. Do we not need more power over others when we feel none within ourselves? Of course, this introduces the paradox that manifests itself in many relationships, the power of the powerless over the powerful. Later in the book we examine the origins of this paradox in the toddler's attempts to control the mother, and the repertoire of controlling strategies that people devise such as seduction, bribery, coercion, and reason.

If one is to look through the indexes of various books on psychoanalytic theory and practice, one is not likely to find the word "power" listed there. Omnipotence, on the other hand, is a concept that is central to the understanding of infantile development and adult psychopathology.

Power *is* a focus of the social psychologist, however. It seems strange, since power is such a central aspect of social behavior, that psychoanalysis has not paid closer attention to it as a facet of human development that should be looked at in its own right.

Jerome Frank (1987) says outright that "I have become convinced that the fundamental psychological impetus to the nuclear arms race is national leaders' drive for power" (p. 337). He cites Metternich (1880) who described Napoleon who "having but one passion, that of power, never lost his time or his means on those objects which might have diverted him from his aim" (p. 281).

Frank notes that issues of power and submission are evident throughout human society. Each social system, with its own values and structures, lays down rules about the distribution of power, defines goals toward which power is directed, provides incentives for exerting power and for submitting to it, and defines what are acceptable or unacceptable methods of applying power.

In view of Frank's observations, one can only deduce that power, along with its interpersonal ramifications, must indeed have its origins in the individual human psyche. To what extent have all societies, from the most primitive to the most complex, had to dedicate themselves to the taming and channeling of this intrinsic "will to power"?

Freud observed this need to tame and channel with respect

to aggression, which he considered an instinctual drive. However, it seems useful to consider power as distinct from aggression, inasmuch as they are subjectively and experientially different from each other. People do not say that they feel good when they can be aggressive. They say they feel good when they can experience themselves as powerful. Indeed, they will either bear the guilt of aggression in order to feel powerful, or bear the shame of powerlessness in order not to be aggressive.

Adolf Hitler took the ideas of Nietzsche, as well as those of Darwin who had observed in nature what he called "the survival of the fittest," to justify the most malevolent use of power in all of human history. To observe the prevalence of the power motive is not the same as to condone or advocate the unbridled yielding to that motive without the intervention of values, conscience, or basic human decency.

However we think about power, as good or bad, as something we want or do not want, there is wide agreement that it is something to be reckoned with at all levels of human behavior— private, interpersonal and social. At the level of the individual, what I refer to as *intrinsic power* sets the stage for how we experience and relate to power in the world at large.

2

Intrinsic Power: The Power of the Self

Self-reverence, self-knowledge,
self-control,
These three alone lead life to
sovereign power.

(Alfred, Lord Tennyson: Oenone)

Every natural power exhilarates;
A true talent delights the
possessor first.

(Ralph Waldo Emerson: The Scholar)

Intrinsic power, the power of the self, refers to a sense of mastery, of competence, of potency in one's dealings with the world of things and with the world of people. There is a sense of being effective, of having an impact, of mattering. It is the power to think, to feel, to know—to experience the creative workings of the mind. It is the power that comes with access to one's own will, with a secure sense of one's self and of one's legitimate place in the world and in one's relationships—a sense of being a grown-up in a world of grown-ups and of knowing that the only secret is that there is no secret.

Those who fully and unconflictedly experience their intrinsic power have their feet firmly planted in reality, in contrast to those who try to live out a fantasy existence of illusion—of a grandiosity

and omnipotence that cover over an *alter-state* of worthlessness
and helplessness. Real power transcends the whim of chance or of
fortune, enabling the individual to persevere and even triumph
through adversity.

The threads of will and power are closely intertwined, and
the commonly used term "willpower" reveals the intuitive understanding of their linkage. A third thread, that of aggression, may
complicate issues of will and power. The *feeling* of having power,
as a feeling, belongs to the realm of the emotions, although it
often is experienced at the bodily level as well. More precisely,
the *emotion* that goes with the *experience* of power is likely to be
elation, a kind of "high." Carried to a pathological extreme, this
would become the high of a manic state, with its associated sense
of omnipotence.

Emerson notes that "every natural power exhilarates." Is
not that exhilaration the feeling of being powerful itself? Having a
sense of mastery and competence not only makes a person feel
good about himself or herself, which is essentially a judgment and
an enhanced self-esteem; it *feels* good in and of itself. Creative
artists speak of the "high" that is experienced when the creative
forces within them spill forth, when the poem just "seems to write
itself." A sense of intrinsic power comes from access to our own
creative spirit.

Will is more closely tied to what is referred to as "intentionality," and has a cognitive, or ideational, component. To say,
"I intend to do such and such," implies the will to do it. It is
something one can articulate with words, that one can think
about; it is a course of action decided upon and the determination
to see it through. Will is an attribute of the self that is determined
to express or assert its own nature. It is the taken for granted
thrust for life that we see in the baby who, just learning to walk,
falls down and doggedly gets up and tries again. The sense of
mastery that comes from the successful expression of will leads to
that feeling referred to here as intrinsic power. Obviously, for one
to live in a social world, will has to be tempered not only with

reality-testing but with concern for others and for the society itself. Some parents see in this necessity a call to "break the child's will" at that point of development when it comes more clearly into conflict with the wishes of the parents. Unfortunately, to break the child's will is to break the child.

Aggression, in contrast to both will and power, has unfortunately acquired a bad name, since it is all too often used to express negative feelings and may be directed against others in a hurtful manner. But in its purest sense, aggression is merely an impulse toward action. The child may have the will to reach out for a nearby toy. The *act* of reaching for it is a manifestation of his healthy aggression, his ability to *go toward* the aim of his intent. A positive marriage of will and aggression is necessary for a person to be effective in the world. Aggression can literally be experienced at the physiological and muscular levels. Moreover, it may take physical energy to *stop* an impulse toward action, as well as to initiate one.

If one is frightened by the impulse, especially when there is anger or rage behind it, or if one feels guilty because of the nature of the motive behind it, he or she may guard against such an impulse by repudiating intention, by denying the wish, and by inhibiting the will. Feelings of powerlessness and anxiety will be a consequence of these inhibitions, and with them one's self-esteem and self-respect will also suffer. The pride of intrinsic power will give way to the shame of its absence. This is not to imply that it is desirable to act upon every impulse. What is desirable is an adequate knowledge about one's own perhaps-hidden conflicts and motives so that, rather than simply inhibiting will, one is able to make conscious choices based upon judgment and values.

Intrinsic power can only be experienced by an authentic or true self, and requires a secure sense of identity. Shulman (1987) marks the distinction between what he views as the *pre-intentional* force of the infant who does not yet have a conscious awareness of the self as an agent with choice; and the *will*, which is a manifestation of the awareness of an "I" who wants or wishes or intends.

Later I will describe how the "I will" is tied to the sense of "I am." Intrinsic power can best be stated in terms of "I am," "I can" and "I will"; that is, in terms of *identity, mastery,* and *intentionality.* People who do not have a clear sense of their own identity often report that they do not know what they want, that they feel as though they have no will of their own. Distortions of identity lead to a loss of intrinsic power. It may be replaced by illusory power that is destructive in its expression, or that becomes essential as a protection against a terrifying awareness of the fragility or helplessness that goes with a poorly defined identity.

Stensrud (1979) writes about personal power from a Taoist perspective. He says, "Personal power is not something we have, but something we live. It is not something we acquire or teach, but something that is a natural part of our nature. Either we experience our personal power as part of an expressive and receptive process, or we do not experience it at all" (p. 39).

He also notes the Taoist belief that "When there is no need to have power or gain credit, when there is no fear that we will lose our power and therefore cling to it, when we can be totally quiet . . . we have all the power we need" (p. 39).

Even with a secure sense of identity, will, and intrinsic power, sooner or later the individual comes face to face with formal power—with the power of parents, of teachers, of policemen, and of government. And between intrinsic and formal power lies the less clearly defined realm of attributed power.

3

Attributed and Formal Power

Attributed Power

Power may be more in the eye of the beholder, something that is *attributed* to the other even when the other feels quite devoid of it. When we look at a newborn infant and its mother, we know that she literally has the power of life and death over it, whereas the baby is the epitome of helplessness and powerlessness. "Not so!" the parents of the baby might reply. "That eight-pound tyrant has destroyed all order in our life. We haven't slept for more than an hour at a stretch since we brought him home from the hospital." Winnicott (1986) noted the power of the baby's appearance of helplessness, a power that renders the parent helpless to resist. Because of their love and concern for their child, parents choose to yield to its needs. Obviously this is necessary for the well-being of the child, but the parents may have deep feelings about it if they have unresolved power conflicts of their own. A parent who murders the baby that cannot be stopped from crying may be expressing the rage of his or her own intensely felt powerlessness of the moment. The power struggle that may take place between parents and their 2-year-old are legend. But more about this later.

Children, unbeknownst to them, often wield parental power over their own parents because of the kinds of conscious and unconscious attributions made by the parents to what the child does or says. Rejection by a small son or daughter can have exactly the same emotional impact on the parent as did rejection by his or her mother or father in the past, evoking the same anxiety, rage, or depression. A spouse, in particular, may be experienced as having power over an individual just as though he or she were a parent. This situation is common because of people's readiness to bring dependency needs into the intimate adult relationship. In the language of psychoanalysis, this process of attribution is referred to as "transference." It often takes place within the patient–therapist interaction in which its examination and exploration enables the individual to understand how he or she "transfers" into current adult relationships the feelings, beliefs, wishes, or fears—as well as strategies for managing relationships with significant others—from formative past relationships. The understanding of how these came to be does not have as its goal the assignment of blame, or what some call "parent-bashing." It is to understand how these feelings, beliefs, wishes, fears, and strategies came to be built into the individual's adult character and how they are now central to the very problems that bring that person into therapy.

On the other hand, power may be arrogated to the self in an equally unrealistic manner. Delusions of grandeur are an obvious and extreme example of this. The anorexia nervosa patient carries feelings of omnipotence to the extreme. The denial of the need to eat is delusional in nature. It is a metaphor for the denial of the need for the other person, of *any* other person, because the other (usually the parent) is experienced as psychologically toxic in one way or another. When parental power is felt to be malevolent, the child may hold on to an illusory omnipotence as a basis for security. More subtle and more common are secret, hidden beliefs about a powerful self who needs nothing from anyone else, a stance that is assisted by convictions of the superior ability, wisdom, or morality of a perfect self. The perfectionism associated with eating disorders often bolsters an illusory defensive grandiose self.

Some people need others to be inadequate in order to main-

tain their illusory power and perfection. This role may be assigned
to the child in the dysfunctional family, or, in other cases, to one
of the marital pair. They become the "containers" of helplessness
and inadequacy for the parent or the spouse. Then the person
who has projected his or her feelings of powerlessness or inadequacy into the "container" can feel powerful and competent. The
child who serves as a container in this fashion is blocked in its own
social, emotional, and intellectual growth.

Whether attributed power is assigned to the self or to the
other, it will inevitably disrupt significant interpersonal relationships. Negative feelings will be stirred up, be they resentment,
envy, or fear.

Formal Power

The objective power of the government or its agents, such as a
policeman, or that of one's teacher or employer, is referred to as
formal power. These individuals are designated to be the holders
of power by virtue of title or position. The ultimate goal of designated or formal power is to enable a social system to operate in a
coordinated manner toward the achievement of shared purposes.
The word "anarchy" refers to the absence of any form of political
authority and is associated with disorder and confusion. Spinoza
noted that we hand over power to a sovereign in return for a
restraint upon the anarchy which threatens all possibility of peace
and survival. This view of formal power addresses the degree to
which it is *designated* and to which it ultimately resides in those
who hand it over, a view consistent with a democratic form of
government. Those governments whose formal power is also absolute render their citizens powerless, a situation that generates
envy and hatred of the state and an inclination to steal or overthrow that power.

In these instances, as is the case of parents and their small
children, there will be moral and philosophical issues with respect

to the use or abuse of power. Can there be such a thing as a "benevolent dictatorship"? What happens to the political "child" or to the child in such a family?

Differing views with respect to values and philosophies in this domain underlie conflict at every level of social organization. Unfortunately, those with designated, or formal, power may in some instances inflate that power with their personal illusory omnipotence or their wish for it. At that point, leadership may take on a messianic zeal that endangers the common good. The charismatic leader uses a combination of attributed and formal power to move people to doing what he wants them to do even though such action may be against their own best interests. The example of Jim Jones and the catastrophe at Jonestown, Guyana in 1978 stands out, where the power of the pulpit gave legitimacy to a leader's personal persuasion.

A well-known sports figure said that if he weren't a player, he would like to have the power that goes with a police uniform. "You know when you're driving down the street and you see maniacs driving around? I'd like to have that power, driving that squad car and wearing that uniform to stop those people. I wish I could pull a guy over and give him a ticket or throw him in a squad car and take him to the station" (*Los Angeles Times* July 19, 1987).

The person who made these statements showed how readily a need for personal power can find a route of formal power in order to express it. Of course, for some people this situation is a set-up for the abuse of formal power. Maybe the culprit would be thrown into the squad car with more force than was necessary.

In the more ordinary situation of day-to-day life, certain kinds of attributed power affect the attitude and behavior of an individual toward the holders of formal power. Anger toward an overbearing father, for example, is transferred inappropriately to one's employer, leading to work difficulties with a failure to succeed in the job or to being fired. Attributed power carries with it beliefs and emotions and motives that affect not only relationships with formal authority, but social and intimate relationships as well. A successful lawyer noted how much power he gave to people who had "family money." "I give them a power they intrinsically do not have. Money does give a certain degree of power, but I give more to it."

In Carl Sagan's novel *Contact* (1985) he writes of Ellie, the central character:

> . . . in conversation with him why was she always accomodating—and argumentative only in extremis? A part of her evidently felt that the granting of her doctorate and the opportunity to pursue her science were still possibilities firmly in Drumlin's hands. [p. 193]

In fact, Ellie was already a world-famous scientist and adviser to the president, while Drumlin was a former professor. In this case the formal power of the teacher became overlaid with the attributed power of a parental figure. In Ellie's experience, even when the formal power had been dissolved, the attributed power remained.

For many individuals, the graduation ceremony does little to change the experience of the self as a child in a world of adults. The evolution of power in the individual and his or her relationship to the power of others, leads to certain patterns of power attribution that complicate adult life. When parents are unwilling to relinquish their formal power in keeping with the development of their child's intrinsic power, a situation evolves that produces envy in the child.

Part II

The Origins of Power and Power Conflicts in Early Development

The Birth of Power: From Attachment to Separation

From an "object relations" point of view, we seek to discover the nature of the unconscious mind that most directly affects the experience of the self, the experience of the other, and the complex relationships between them.

A developmental approach to the understanding of these experiences of self and other, experiences that include ideas, perception, feelings, wishes, and impulses, has taken us back further and further in the life of the child. Most recent research highlights the interactional basis of their evolution from the start of life. The human newborn's readiness to respond to, as well as to initiate, that interaction is as genetically patterned as the hunting and mating behavior of other species. And built into the healthy central nervous system is the readiness to respond to patterns and actively to construct and synthesize new ones.

The patterning of the mental schema we call "self," and the patterning of the mental schema referred to as the "object," take place in predictable, hierarchical stages. We use the term "object" rather than "mother" because this particular mental image is in part *created by* the child in accord with his or her limited mental capabilities, and with his or her own unique experience of the early care-taking environment. In a way, the child creates a kind of metaphor or template for the significant other from his or her interpersonal experiences. In turn this metaphor, or template, reciprocally shapes the child's perception of and expectations of the interpersonal environment, along with his or her behavior toward it. Through its genetically endowed intrinsic creative capacities, its inborn intrinsic power, the infant creates an inner image of its self as well. "Object relations" refers to the dynamic interplay between the inner images of both self and other. This interplay entails the perception and experience of power *along* with feelings, wishes, thoughts and impulses.

As the child negotiates a series of development processes—beginning with that of attachment—each process brings him or her to a higher level of structural organization. The self and object images, referred to in psychoanalytic terms as self and object representations, become increasingly complex, and increasingly differentiated from one other. Each level of psychic organization determines to a large extent the nature of the child's experience of himself and of the other, along with their characteristic interaction. The experience of power and the knowledge of where it is located, and of how it affects feelings about the self and about relationships, are integral aspects of this organization.

The Balance of Power

We're accustomed to the term, *balance of power,* within the context of international relations. There is also a balance of power within the context of interpersonal relationships. Sometimes this balance is defined rigidly in a one-sided manner, with the submissive participant accumulating a store of negative feelings about the situation. Sometimes there are battles as to which will be the powerful one, battles in which there must be a loser as well as a winner. In a healthier relationship, power is shared in an agreed-upon manner that does not imply defeat or humiliation for the one who may willingly cede power to the other on the basis of genuine respect or confidence and/or the exigencies of the moment. For example, if one partner in such a relationship bears the responsibility of writing and balancing the checkbook, it is not to control economic resources, nor does the other partner feel controlled. If one partner is under stress and in need of support from the other, the one who is needed is in a position of greater power at that moment. He or she uses the situation not to gain an advantage over the other, but to enable the other to recover and to feel secure in his or her own intrinsic power as well as in the ability and safety to turn to the other when times are difficult. And it is possible in such a relationship to acknowledge you are wrong without being humiliated. U.S. Secretary of State George R. Schultz noted that *sharing* power is more difficult than exercising power. It requires an attitude of trust and safety to relinquish it when one has it as well as to be able to bear not having it.

People who say yes when they want to say no, and people who say no when they want to say yes, are often people who still struggle with unresolved issues around the balance of power in interpersonal situations.

There will be, for most people, a predictable evolution of this balance of power, although a particular child's evolution may go awry when the parent's need for power blocks this healthy evolution.

The subtleties of the power balance and power conflict within the family is described in an example given by Boszormenyi-Nagy and Framo (1965). They paint a picture of a family situation "in which a father blusters and talks a great deal trying to establish his position as head of the household, and his wife, at the end of the hour, by an almost imperceptible gesture or phrase, negates the thousands of words of her husband, reduces him to raging or quiet impotence, and quickly re-establishes her power" (pp. 425–426). The father's behavior appeared to be dominant, but the real power was in the hands of the apparently passive wife.

The authors describe research that shows the difference between schizophrenic and "normal" family groups. The discriminating factor was not with whom the authority rested, but whether it would be shared without conflict. Power issues are often at the core of family and individual pathology. Who is weak and who is strong is always at question, and one person can be in positions of powerlessness and omnipotence at the same time. In the case of a child who has to contain and personify the parent's projected powerlessness so the parent can feel powerful, the child feels he or she is omnipotently in control of that parent's emotional well-being.

The balance, as it exists between a child and its parents, begins with real power in the hands of the parents, and particularly in the hands of the primary caretaker. The power of the infant is largely illusory and comes from the parent's response to the baby's cries, a response that allows a sense of effectiveness to develop in the child. This sense of effectiveness, of having an impact, of being able to evoke a helpful response, is one of the seeds of intrinsic power that develops over the early years of life. Other seeds of intrinsic power may be there as givens, as part of the child's genetic and constitutional endowment. They are, however, as yet undeveloped and unevolved in the young child. These are the intrinsic capacities for will and for healthy, unconflicted aggression—that is, the capacity to *move toward* what it wants. Nevertheless, the balance of power weighs heavily on the side of the parent at the beginning of life.

The Preattachment Stage

At birth the child is endowed with attachment-seeking behaviors to which the mother responds under normal circumstances. Although built-in precursors of self and object images are present in the form of the child's innately determined responses to the human environment, the experiences and the patterning that lead to enduring and evolving memory traces require time to become established in the infant's mind. The baby needs to have a mental image of the mother that can be maintained in her absence in order to be able to miss her, to have a feeling of specifically wanting her.

Piaget (1955) studied the development of what he called "object permanence." According to his research, at 6 or 7 months of age, a baby will look for something he has dropped if he wants to play with it, but he will only look for a very short time. Then the baby seems to forget about it. By 8 or 9 months of age, the child will continue to search for something that is no longer in view—remembering it and remembering that he wants it. It is at this age that babies develop acute separation anxiety and separation distress as well as fear of strangers. They have an image of the mother firmly in mind and attach to that image their feelings of security and well-being.

Some people who defensively deny wanting or wishing for an important other do so because they cannot tolerate the feelings of powerlessness resulting from not being able to control another. Such a feeling may evoke unbearable frustration and rage. In effect, they wipe out the image of the important other, in order to avoid these painful emotions.

A conscious awareness of intrinsic power will develop out of the constitutional givens—that is, the innate potential for will and healthy aggression, or moving-toward, as well as the genetic endowment that will lead to the gradual unfolding of perception, intellect, and motility. Quite probably, the experience of power that exists in the very first months of life will come closest to that of the Taoist view; that it is not something we acquire, but something that is a natural part of our nature.

The Process of Attachment and the Stage of Symbiosis

Over the earliest months of life we see the innate attachment-seeking behavior of the infant interacting with maternal behavior and response in a manner that, optimally, brings about what Margaret Mahler (Mahler et al. 1975) refers to as the stage of symbiosis when the child's inner self-image is linked to that of the mother. At this point of development, around the fourth or fifth month of life, the child has synthesized experiences of him or herself in such a way as to create an enduring image that includes the primary caretaker and the salient qualities of their characteristic interaction. It is at this point that the basis for an affectional relationship and for what Erik Erikson (1950) calls "basic trust" is laid down. The mother's emotional availability and her capacity for empathic response is essential to this process.

A sense of power comes from the experience of oneness in which the power of the self and that of the other are in total harmony rather than in opposition. Before the enduring mental image of the primary caretaker becomes secure in memory, it is likely that the child will be aware of power issues only when that harmony is disturbed and the child is thrust into a state of helplessness. Rage and terror will accompany this kind of basic powerlessness. There will have to be an enduring mental image of the mothering person—an image that is understood as separate from the self—before there can be a *perception* of her as powerful.

Imagine you are a small baby, perhaps 2 or 3 months old. You have just awakened and are becoming restless as the pangs of hunger grip you with increasing strength. You cannot get up and go to the refrigerator. You can't get up and go into the kitchen, where your mother is preparing dinner for the family to tell her you are ready for something to eat *NOW*. Your whimpers and now your cries have not yet been heard or responded to.

What can better epitomize powerlessness than this situation? You are powerless to make yourself feel good and you are powerless over the external environment, until and unless some other who has the power to give or to withold, to comfort or to abandon, chooses to respond to your intense need.

Then, miraculously, a familiar face appears and a familiar voice is heard. You are lifted and cradled in her arms, and before long you are nestled against her soft warmth and familiar smell, and free to take as much as you need. Powerlessness and helplessness are gone, and your mother's power has magically become your own.

The child's first sense of his or her own power thus comes

largely from sharing the power of the primary caretaker to whom it is emotionally bonded. Usually this is the mother. When she uses her real power in the service of the physical and emotional well-being of her small child, that child develops both a basic trust in the world around it and a basic security with respect to its own existence.

Winnicott (1987) notes how "the adapting mother presents the world in such a way that the baby starts with a ration of the *experience of omnipotence* . . ." He also notes how, in certain mental illnesses, omnipotence is asserted by means of delusions. In these cases, he tells us, a self had to be created by that child without the help of a mother who adapts to its needs. The primacy of the role of the mother in the evolution of the power dimension of human experience was articulated by a woman who said, "Mothers can make life okay in ways a father can't touch. Mothers can obliterate you. Fathers can't define you in such a fundamental way."

The scenario of achieving power by sharing that of someone else who is perceived of in an idealized manner, to whom both omnipotence and perfection are attributed, can become the template for all later power arrangements. However, it is a quasi-symbiosis that will inevitably be problematic. Later in life, in the repetition of achieving a sense of power through participation in another's omnipotence and perfection, through attaching oneself to the powerful other, the individual is in a precarious position if the other does not fulfill expectations. Furthermore, the other may come to feel the burden of these expectations and may come to resent them, also fearing the ready rage that will come his or her way from the dependent partner who feels disillusioned and disappointed.

In one such situation, when Tom Jordan's expected promotion did not come through, instead of being able to support him through what was his own career crisis, his wife Evelyn became enraged at him. She blamed him for his failure to maintain the illusory pride she experienced through her identity as his wife, by virtue of which she felt that she took on his prestige and power.

The quality of the child's experience during the attachment process, and during subsequent separations, losses, and disappointments in the first three years of life, will build into the child's inner world certain characteristic feelings and expectations about the interpersonal world, and will color subsequent developmental stages. These feelings and expectations will include the child's sense of power or powerlessness in regard to the primary caretaker.

No sooner is the symbiotic structure of a merged image of self and object established than the child moves toward a new process, that of separation and individuation (Mahler et al. 1975).

Moving toward Separateness and Individuality

The satisfactory "symbiotic" emotional milieu sets the stage for a positive relationship to the intrinsic power of the self, and toward relationships with others in whom power is vested. Both a sense of security and a positive self-esteem begin to develop concomitantly, the self-esteem being tied to intrinsic power, the security being tied to trust and faith in significant others. Thus power, from the start, is an essential element of both security and self-esteem.

The beginnings of intrinsic power will remain with the child as he or she gradually separates out from the interpersonal matrix of the mother–child dyad as a unique, individual self, and will facilitate that development. There will be a sense of the intrinsic power of the self, as well as security in being able to feel safely dependent on parental figures, being able to value and look up to the power attributed to them without envying it or wanting to destroy it or steal it from them.

Over time, intrinsic power will come to play an increasingly greater role in the maintenance of both security and self-esteem, eventually taking over the lion's share of responsibility for those feelings. This recalls the comment of one participant in my inquiry, that "Power is the ability to control your own state of emotional well-being." But this does not mean that in the healthiest course of life, one will not, from time to time, and when under stress, feel the need for support or advice or comfort from someone else. However, because of the fundamental strengths that are secure within the healthy person's own psyche, it will be possible to turn to others without undue anxiety or shame.

This capacity for healthy emotional autonomy comes from the child's internalization, making part of the self the good parenting that once was supplied from outside. In psychoanalytic terms, this is referred to as having achieved "object constancy." The good, reliable caretakers who reflect to the child their love and esteem for him or her, and for that child's intrinsic power, provide a nutriment that gradually becomes part of the child's own internal feelings from within himself or herself.

With the awareness of separateness from the primary caretaker to whom the child had become emotionally bonded, the child can no longer sustain the illusion of oneness with the mother and of magical participation in her power. With intellectual development, the child is confronted with the reality of his or her smallness and dependency on the mother who now, along with the father, takes on the character of an authority figure rather than one of a quasi-extension of the self.

As the child begins to "hatch" out of its undifferentiated self-object experience, it is still profoundly dependent on the mother to provide a sense of wholeness and safety. Eight-month separation anxiety reflects the dependency that the baby still feels toward the primary caretaker to whom it is emotionally bonded. Although other attachments are also developing, as to the father and perhaps to a substitute caretaker, the security of the self is still most closely tied to the primary attachment figure.

From about 10 to 16 months of age, the child's focus shifts increasingly to those "autonomous" functions that develop as a consequence of the maturation of the central nervous system—such functions as locomotion, perception, and the learning process, including the acquisition of language and the understanding of concepts. The child is also increasingly confronted with the experience of its real separateness from the mother. Her ready availability when she is needed and the pleasure the child derives from the mastery of new abilities, make these small separations tolerable for the child. These new abilities form the basis for a conscious awareness of intrinsic power. This includes the elation of being able to stand upright and then to walk alone. Mahler and colleagues (1975) describe the time of this achievement as the peak point of the child's belief in his own magic omnipotence, but says that it is still to a considerable degree derived *"from his sense of sharing in his mother's magic powers"* (p. 20).

Learning to walk, discovering spatial relationships, and mastering the remarkable invention of language—all of which captivate and capture the mother—contribute to the child's conscious experience of his or her own power. *"Andrew* do it! *Andrew* do it!" The child's insistence on doing it himself, and the elation and pride that go with mastery of small, yet monumental, tasks are characteristic of the intrinsic power noted by Emerson.

Echoes of what is called the "practicing period" and its magic omnipotence sometimes lead to persisting beliefs about the magical nature of one's abilities and powers. Learning to walk and talk do indeed come as if by magic, unlike the conscious effort one must make to learn the vocabulary of a foreign language at school. I have worked with some individuals who were clearly of superior intelligence and to whom learning had been effortless throughout their education. Paradoxically, they were far less secure about their abilities than people of lesser innate ability. They didn't have the sense of conscious effort through the use of their own actual abilities, which gives one a feeling of some connection with and control over what one can and cannot do. What comes by magic can also disappear by magic. One cannot reply upon it. People who learn so easily—as if by magic—are especially vulnerable to feelings of powerlessness and shame. They may develop a defensive, illusory sense of power that temporarily counteracts these unpleasant feelings, but illusion is unreliable and there is likely to be a chronic underlying anxiety.

The seeds of grandiosity and omnipotence, an inflated sense of one's own power, are generated during the practicing period along with the abilities that emerge by virtue of neurological maturation and learning. Dreams of flying are sometimes reminiscent of the experience of standing upright for the first time. At that moment the baby's eye level is raised above that of the creeping or crawling position. The whole world looks different at this breathtaking elevation. That sense of omnipotence and grandiosity may be recalled and reactivated later in life as a way to deal with intolerable feelings of worthlessness or powerlessness. It will always be available as a defense, whether to a pathological and fantasy-dominated degree, or in its milder form of bragging about one's accomplishments. One of my patients expressed fear of his sense of innate creativity because "it feeds into my feelings of omnipotence."

Toward the latter half of the second year of life, the child reaches a critical switch point. It is here that power struggles may emerge in full bloom. Many adults continue to fight for control in their interpersonal relationships because of unresolved issues left over from "the power pivot."

5

The Rapprochement Phase and the Rapprochement Crisis

Around the age of 18 months, the toddler becomes increasingly and consciously aware of its separateness and differentness from its mother, and of her separateness and differentness from him or her. The child's experiences with reality have counteracted any overestimation of omnipotence, self-esteem has been deflated, and the child is especially vulnerable to shame. Furthermore, the child's dependence upon the mother—who is now perceived as the powerful one—confronts the child with his or her relative helplessness. There is an upsurge of separation anxiety, and the child is more prone to depressed moods. If the mother or another caretaker uses power in a benign and helpful manner, that power is the basis for the child's sense of security and self-esteem. If, on the other hand, parental power is experienced as being against the self, as being something that is not only given but also withheld, the child may come to both hate and envy that power and will develop his or her own techniques to control it. Behind such controlling behavior lies insecurity and anxiety. A businessman commented on how big and scary a father must look to a little boy, "and more so if he's not told he is loved. The big guy has to hold the little one to make him feel protected and loved."

The response of parents and older siblings to the toddler's emerging power are critical in determining his or her relationship to budding intrinsic power. Do they beam and say, "Good for you!" or, "Daniel did it all by himself. What a big boy!" when he tries to tie his own shoelaces? Or do they find his wish to do it himself a nuisance that merely extends the time necessary to get ready to go to the store? Do they find his need for what Kohut (1971) referred to as "mirroring" to be an irritating demand on time and attention? Or are they merely indifferent to it?

The parent who actively interferes with the child's attempts at mastery, who regularly and characteristically overrides the child's expression of will and its intrinsic power, may condition such expression negatively, sending a message that it is undesirable. Some children are more passive and accommodating and will give up their emerging power in order to secure their relationship with the needed other. These children will gain interpersonal power by assuring parental approval through compliance. In this situation, power over the other will become more important than the relinquished intrinsic power of the self.

Some children will have tantrums and insist on doing what they want to do, and the classic power struggle between parents and the 2-year-old is set in motion. To the degree that parents who hold the ultimate power are willing to share it *appropriately,* allowing for necessary setting of limits and socialization, they reinforce the child's intrinsic power in a positive way.

When parents are conflicted about having power, and thus are in conflict about exercising it appropriately in their parental role, they may vascillate between guilty passivity, submitting to the tyranny of their small child, and angry aggression against the child. They will be unable to maintain a consistent firmness when such firmness in limit-setting is required. Under these circumstances, the little boy or girl develops a parallel conflict, with anxiety and guilt at having overthrown the parent alongside rage at having been aggressed upon. Alternating between frightening feelings of omnipotence with its apparent power to destroy, and feelings of helplessness and humiliation, the child cannot develop a realistic and healthy sense of intrinsic power. As an adult, he or she will be caught up in the same love-destroying power cycle as were the parents earlier in life.

Some children who do not meet with anyone's "good for you!" withdraw into themselves and find power within a fantasy world. Sometimes the seeds of health become embedded in pathological behavior and will later have to be freed up to be expressed in more appropriate ways.

Erik Erikson (1950) speaks of the developmental task of the second year of life, which is to achieve autonomy and thus to avoid the development of shame and doubt. He notes how shaming a child "exploits an increasing sense of being small, which can develop only as the child stands up and as his awareness permits him to note the relative measures of size and power" (p. 123).

The first major thrust towards a change in the child's relationship to the power of the parents comes in the second year of life. This is not to say that the child does not have a mind of its own from the very start of life. Indeed, it does. Child development research indicates the considerable extent to which an infant is the initiator of social interaction and follows its own interest in the nonhuman external world, as when it reaches for a brightly colored toy or turns its head and listens intently to a ticking clock. As already noted, intentionality and will, as well as aggression, are there from the very start, constituting the atoms that eventually make up the molecule of intrinsic power. They will become increasingly important and apparent as the child moves toward greater separateness from the mother and inevitably loses the early illusion of omnipotence. As the child is faced with its realistic dependency on the mother whose power is also perceived more realistically, albeit still in an idealized fashion, the stage is set for the power struggles of the second year of life.

In *Being and Loving* I referred to this developmental switch point as "the power pivot," the point at which the child loses its infantile illusions of power and comes face-to-face with the reality of dependency on powerful parental figures. Speak to the parents of most 2-year-olds and you are likely to hear stories of daily power struggles around the minutest aspects of interaction. The child may protest any act of initiative on the part of its mother.

The patience of parents can be sorely tried and they may react angrily and punitively. On the other hand, out of some misdirected wish to support the child's initiative and autonomy, they may submit to the child's tyranny. Unfortunately, instead of leading to self-confidence, this is more likely to generate anxiety-provoking beliefs of unrealistic power and an ability to overpower or destroy the parent on whom the child is really so dependent.

The major concern of the individual who struggles with issues associated primarily with this stage of development is the loss of the support, love, and approval of the other. It is a time when the child may come to believe, for one reason or another, that assertion of his or her own will must lead to such loss. Out of anxiety over this, the child may develop a way of being with others based on submission or compliance, a state of chronic powerlessness and shame, in order to be sure of the continued support and love of the powerful other. This persisting dependent way of seeing the self and the other, and the expectations and demands that go with it, tend to put a strain on interpersonal relationships. Although the other may be idealized, he or she is also feared and envied because of the perceived power and is blamed when things do not go well.

The response of the environment to the child's growth has to allow for its conflicting strivings toward autonomy side by side with the intensely felt dependency needs. The term "rapprochement" suggests the moving away from the mother alternating with the return to her for emotional refueling. Healthy parents do not have a need for the child either to stay dependent and helpless, or to be completely self-reliant. In less satisfactory situations, the child either has to be the container of powerlessness and shame for the parents, or has to develop an illusory sense of power in order to defend against the anxieties of being shoved "out of the nest" prematurely.

The relationship to the power of authority figures who are clearly separate from the self evolves through a series of developmental steps, culminating with the achievement of certain developmental tasks of adolescence. This shift is susceptible to considerable conflict and some people are unable to negotiate these developmental challenges, remaining perennial children in regard to parental figures, perennial protegés to mentors, or perennial students to teachers. Others, reacting rebelliously against authority and its power, are equally unresolved with respect to these conflicts.

Echoes of the rapprochement crisis are heard in adolescence, and conflicts and anxieties left over from this earlier developmental stage will affect the manner in which the young person negotiates the later developmental tasks. Anxiety over self-assertion, whether of the expression of will or even of intrinsic power, will make it difficult for that boy or girl to take the necessary steps toward moving out of the parental home.

The Flight from Power

Madison Avenue knows the selling power of power itself. The maker of a well-known computer tells the prospective buyer, "You will have the *power*—the power to be your best!" Such words draw upon the appeal of intrinsic power.

More familiar are commercials for automobiles, commercials that radiate a promise of the power imbued by a powerful car. This is a form of conferred power, power attributed to the self by virtue of association with a powerful other. The power associated with the powerful car is often thought to have greater appeal to males, and jokes are made about its phallic significance.

There are people who are afraid to drive because of the power associated with automobiles. They are afraid their power might get out of control. This fear is often a derivative of a deeper and older fear, that one's aggression and power will be used against the parents in a destructive manner. This fear is often a concomitant of intense anger at the parents, often for their misuse of power vis-à-vis the child.

Whether we are speaking of interpersonal relationships, or of achievement in one's chosen field, or of the freedom to be unrestrictedly creative, a fear of being powerful generates defenses that ensure its opposite. Various forms of self-sabotage are commonly conceived of as stemming from a "fear of success." This explanation, while perhaps true, is far too vague to be of use in bringing about change. We must ask, what is our definition of success? What are the unconscious implications of that success? What are the underlying wishes, feelings, impulses, and beliefs that are associated with being successful? As a patient said:

"I don't know what it is to be a woman and to be powerful. I'm afraid of the sense of my own power. I discount it and do the opposite. I never even let myself win at tennis. I'm afraid if I'm successful, I'll be destructive. I devastated my brother by being more successful than he. If I outshine my husband, I'll destroy his ego, too."

If we think of success as a form of power, or as a manifestation of power, the fear becomes easier to comprehend. There are four major developmental issues or steps that entail power and that also become conflicted because of fear or guilt about power.

The first of these is that of the "power pivot," when the earlier infantile illusions of omnipotence give way to a more realistic sense of the child's relative helplessness in the world. At the same time, with the emerging conscious perception of the power of the parents, along with the potential for establishing entrenched power struggles in interpersonal relationships, the emotion of *envy* is born.

6

Power and Envy

Envy as a developmental issue is most salient at the point at which the toddler becomes painfully aware that he or she is not omnipotent after all, that the balance of power weighs heavily in favor of the mother, and of the father as well. This marks the beginning of the rapprochement stage of separation and individuation, and contributes to its being a crisis in the life of the child. *Crisis* is defined in the dictionary as the decisive moment, a turning point. The willingness of parents to allow and promote the child's own intrinsic power in terms of adequacy, autonomy, and feelings of mastery, will make it unnecessary for that child to develop illusions of power, compensatory power, or power over others in order to feel good about himself or herself. As one young woman put it, "I like the power in feeling good about myself. I use the word *power* because I feel defenseless in my insecurity."

The connection between power and envy may have something to do with what is viewed as the universality of both. Whereas Nietzsche[1] wrote that "Wherever I found a living creature, there I found the will to power," Hazlitt[2] tells us that "Envy is the most universal passion."

Racker (1957) noted that a prerequisite to envy is a pain-

---

[1] Friedrich Nietzsche, *Thus Spake Zarathustra* (1844–1900).
[2] William Hazlitt, *Characteristics* (1778–1830).

ful recognition that one lacks what the other has. And Sir Francis Bacon[3] observed that "envy is ever joined with the comparison of a man's self; and where there is no comparison, no envy." As an all-consuming passion, it is well described by Antisthenes[4] with the analogy: "As iron is eaten by rust, so are the envious consumed by envy." Envy is a passion not to be envied! Etchegoyen and colleagues (1987) write that envy is "an exquisitely irrational phenomenon, insofar as it pursues no other serviceable end than that of attacking what is valuable in the other, including his capacity of giving it to us." Thus envy generates an ever-increasing sense of frustration and deprivation which is partially self-imposed. It often gets in the way of receiving what is available.

One man noted his envy of his therapist, saying, "I contrast myself with what I think you have, all the things I'd like to achieve. It stops me from taking you as a model, from taking in the positiveaspects, because if I take from you I have to acknowledge that you have, and that only increases the envy." He could not develop himself in a manner that would enhance his sense of intrinsic power and his self-esteem. Instead he would feel passive, powerless, and humiliated.

Although the individual may be reacting in some degree to a realistic frustration, he plays a role in the perpetuation of that frustration far beyond that which may be unavoidable. The parentcertainly has more power realistically than the child, but malignant envy of that power will interfere with a child's capacity to evolve a sense of intrinsic power and of effectiveness in the world. The less benign the use of parental power, the more hatred and envy are likely to develop and the more malignant their role in the person's life. The greater the envy and hatred of parental power, the greater the wish to destroy that power. Conscious or even unconscious murderous impulses toward the parent, who is also needed, inevitably generate guilt and anxiety. A defensive rejec-

---

[3]Sir Francis Bacon, *Of Envy* (1561–1626).
[4]Antisthenes, *Diogenes Laertius* VI (443 B.C.–366 B.C.).

tion of power and a posture of powerlessness may be the outcome. The consequent state of impotence and inferiority then
generates another cycle of envy of the other's power.

Denigrating that which is envied is another technique that
may be used to control the envy itself. This is analogous to the
"sour grapes" defense: We convince ourselves that we do not
want what we cannot have. We also convince ourselves that there
is nothing to envy by spoiling that which is so very enviable from
the individual's unique perspective. Beerbohm[5] wrote that "the
dullard's envy of brilliant men is always assuaged by the suspicion
that they will come to a bad end."

Some women who are envious of the power their husbands
have in the family system, power the woman consciously and
unconsciously attributes to him, or who are envious of the idealized life they imagine their husbands have in the world outside the
home, become critical in a way that aims to destroy him as an
object of envy. These women may also go out of their way to
denigrate and thus spoil him in the eyes of their children. Thus,
being loved by the father makes the children feel shame rather
than pride. This stands as a destructive element in the development of both sons and daughters. He cannot be used as a model
for identification by his son, who then becomes conflicted about
his masculinity because he does not want to be like the devalued
father. The son may choose instead to identify with his powerful
mother, but this endangers his sense of maleness. What the father
may have in general to give his children is rendered worthless.
Meanwhile, the mother feels more powerful, having thoroughly
diminished her envied partner.

Penis Envy

The psychoanalytic concept of "penis envy" is an extreme anath-
ema to a feminist. Perhaps this is partially because of the implica-

---

[5]Max Beerbohm, *Zuleika Dobson* IV.

tion that that which is envied is necessarily superior, which, of course, it need not be. It is, however, superior *in the mind of the envier,* or she would not envy. To her it must be enviable. Whatever the political issues, there are, whether one likes it or not, women who do wish they had a penis—some concretely and some for what it symbolizes *to them.* The man who at some level fears the power of the woman, starting with the early mother who is probably the most powerful figure in his psychological development, may play upon the tendency of some women to idealize the power they attribute to males. Her envy of *his* power is an antidote for his fearful envy of hers.

Nevertheless, and political aspects aside, there are women for whom the envy of the very power they attribute to men— starting with the father, or the brother who was their mother's favorite because he was a boy—becomes expressed metaphorically as penis envy. A woman in therapy notes, "It all comes down to an issue of power and control. I think I'm envious I don't have a cock—that sense of power men have, and the elitism of their sex in society." Another woman alluded to a similar view, speaking of her father: "I could see it in relation to his being male, the envy. I tried to show him as being less. But I'm glad I'm a woman. It's easier. The trying and exerting part of being male is what I don't want. I don't want to be a man, but wish to have that—aggressiveness." Whereas one woman struggles to find her own healthy and intrinsic power so that she does not have to envy men, another chooses the easier path of attaching herself to the powerful man and sharing in his power. Unfortunately, this keeps the latter woman perennially cognizant of her own real sense of powerlessness and perennially envying what she wants her husband to be able to provide.

Power that is associated with *negative* emotions, with fear and hate, is power that is envied. Power that is associated with *positive* emotions, with love and security, is not envied but may be turned to dependently or may serve as a model for achieving one's own power. It does not have to be stolen or overthrown. One woman said to her therapist "I want to be like you when I grow up. Your power seems so quiet and centered." She would come to discover her own intrinsic power, particularly that of her creative mind.

If the envy of power becomes tied to gender-specific qualities, it may take the form of penis envy in women or womb envy in men. The envy becomes "concretized" and the person experiences "organ inferiority." If it is the mother who is powerful and controlling, and the father who is weak, the daughter is not likely to develop penis envy. The battle is then with the mother and with women. Women who have contempt for their fathers, a contempt that is generalized to all men, will probably find the very idea of penis envy ridiculous. The envy of her mother's power is far more disturbing to her development. If the girl hates that power, she does not want to identify with it or to have power of her own lest she be like what she hates in her mother. So she chooses the path of powerlessness which, repetitively, will put her in opposition to and envying and hating the power of others. As much as she may be drawn to powerful women because she devalues weak men, she cannot have a loving relationship with them either. McDougall (1987) reports cases of lesbian women who devoted all their thoughts and energy to their lovers, as they had done with their narcissistic and controlling mothers, and who ended by feeling a covert envy and hatred which threatened the relationship (p. 171).

When the father's power is a source of happiness and pleasure, and the little girl feels wonderful because she feels especially loved by her daddy, she will not want to steal his power or overthrow it. She does not envy it because she shares in it by virtue of her specialness. She will feel positive about being in the passive and receptive position with regard to her father.

As she gets older, however, staying in the passive and receptive position may become a problem for her if this powerless stance permeates her relationships and her way of being in the world. Even if she is able to move past this way of feeling special and powerful—that is, to find other ways than by attaching herself to admired and powerful father figures and making herself special to them—she may continue to enjoy sex more in the passive and receptive position since this way of relating was what became eroticized in the early years. If she cannot move past this way of relating to men, she may eventually come to envy the power she has attributed to them, a power that she once adored.

When male power has been used *against* the girl, penis envy is more apt to develop. One woman noted that she didn't like intercourse unless she could be on top. "I don't want to feel like a submissive victim. I don't want a penis so I can be superior to someone else. I just want to be equal. If you have a sword, I want one too and not just a shield." She recalled how humiliated she used to feel when her abusive brother would pin her down. It was her brother's male power she hated and envied, not her father's.

Spoiling

The man who envies the power of the woman on whom he is emotionally dependent, also envies the power she has over him. His spoiling of her with criticism, his rendering her a "basket case," frees him of his intolerable envy and the feelings of being "less-than" in comparison with her. Unfortunately, once he has rendered her impotent and thus unenviable, he resents the burden she seems to have become. We often see a relationship that begins with the man "putting her on a pedestal." It very soon changes into one of a litany of criticisms of her physical, mental, emotional, and/or spiritual qualities. She whom he has extolled, he must bring down in order to restore his own power and pride.

But as Etchegoyen and colleagues (1987) point out, envy ultimately *must* spoil that which is good. The person who is envied automatically becomes "bad" because of the very fact that he or she produces envy. Thus, what is good is made bad. On the other hand, what is bad and thus not to be envied, paradoxically becomes good. There is a confusion about what is good and what is bad. These writers also observe that the most virulent envy is excited by the powerful, idealized other who can do with impunity what is forbidden to everyone else. The envy of the abusive parent comes about not because he or she is abusive per se, but because he or she has the power to do anything and to get away with it. It is in this paradox that we find one explanation for the fact that a person with such a background may be drawn to abusive and powerful partners. The "weakness" of the good parent makes a potentially good partner undesirable, an essentially "spoiled" other. Father may have been better loved because he was more nurturant, but mother had the power. Since being powerful is more desirable than being weak, love is renounced for power.

The major difference between envy and admiration, which are on opposite ends of a continuum, with both denoting a "looking-up" attitude toward the other, is a belief in the availability to the self of that which is looked up to. The more attainable those qualities or achievements, the more the admired other stands as a model, as a beacon for one's own development. If what is looked up to is in some way forbidden to the self, either by virtue of messages from others or from one's own inability to pursue it, envy will result. Thus, frustration and envy are linked internally if not in actual fact. As Pope[6] noted:

> Envy, to which th' ignoble mind's a slave,
> Is emulation in the learn'd or brave.

A woman in therapy noted that in general she envied her mother for being able to do things she could not. Her mother needed to keep her daughter in an inferior position in order to bolster her own sense of power and worth. However, when her mother was willing to show her how to do something, when she indicated that her daughter could indeed have intrinsic power of her own, "I

---

[6]Alexander Pope, *An Essay on Man II.*

could tolerate her knowing. I didn't envy it," the daughter said. Looking-up then took the form of admiration and emulation rather than envy. The mother's message at these times was that power could be shared.

Envy develops when the balance of power is lopsided, when all the power is kept on one side of the relationship. From the perspective of the powerless partner, the only way to get power may be to destroy the other, or to steal his or her power by a number of covert power-tactics. The concept of sharing power, of recognizing that each person's intrinsic power can be a rich resource in the relationship, may be alien to the individual's history and experience and thus to his or her fundamental beliefs about power in interpersonal relationships. The guilt and anxiety about the conscious or unconscious impulse to steal or destroy may lead to a defensive refusal to have power. This may well exist side-by-side with tactics of power and control that are steadfastly denied, although they certainly have an impact on friends, colleagues, or intimate partners. The self-imposed state of impotence generates further rage, shame, and envy, while covert power tactics generate similar negative feelings in others.

One woman, experiencing her growth and development and the emerging sense of her own power, told me she felt guilty about these changes. She felt this way because she at times envied me and felt competitive with me. She said she felt as though she were either stealing my power or killing *my* powerful self. However, she enjoyed the sense of mastery she had achieved in being able to understand and deal with the problems in her life. It was this sense of mastery that was the essence of her feeling powerful. At these times her motive was not to compete with me, or to show herself as more capable. So often the drive for mastery, for intrinsic power, does get caught up in competitive strivings as well. Under these circumstances, the emotional conflict is all the greater. In her case, the mother's need to be the powerful figure in the family had made it necessary for others to give up their own power. In doing this, the daughter had unconsciously felt that she was protecting her mother from hurt; there was probably some truth to that, insofar as her mother's power was defensive and illusory and covered over deeper feelings of powerlessness and anxiety. This kind of situation in the family puts pressure on those who become the "containers" of inadequacy and powerlessness. They feel terrible about themselves, but they feel they have no choice, that to do otherwise would, in some mysterious way, be wrong, dangerous, or destructive.

A man who had been in psychotherapy off and on over many years explained how he had needed to return to get his "batteries recharged." We spoke of how he experienced power as residing only in the therapist, of the barriers to his having his own power, and of how that would all keep him perpetually dependent on a therapist. The problem that brought him to treatment with me was his failure to be promoted at work. His relationships with those both above and below him in the hierarchy of formal power were intensely conflicted. His inability to act when he should have, or his heavy-handedness when he was in a position of greater power, interfered with the group's achievement of their shared goal.

Another woman commented that to do well at something her father did well would be like betraying him. It would be a threat to his power. She protected both parents by diminishing herself. She had to keep her successes a secret.

The adolescent is confronted in normal development with a parallel conflict. How can one become an adult with his or her own power without doing something bad or hurtful to one or both parents?

A woman who characteristically clung to a powerless position in order to force her mother to take care of her, as well as to protect the mother against the hate of her own envy of the older woman's power, said of an associate, "I hate her, and there's nothing that can be done about it. I spoil her by thinking her seams are crooked, or that she only *seems* nice because she is so shallow. I'm powerless with her. I do want to smash her, to get rid

of her, to tell her what I think of her. And I hate *you* [the thera-
pist] for being so strong. I feel impotent. I can't change you. I'll
kiss ass and walk away hating you. It's a passive ragefulness."

Although she used to think of herself as competitive, she
came to understand the critical difference between competitiveness and envy. This difference resides in the degree of hostility
and the wish to spoil or destroy that go with envy. One can value
the competitive rival and have no wish to harm that person. In
competitiveness, unlike envy, the only wish is to win.

Refusal of Power

Whereas envy leads to a hateful attitude toward those who have
what is believed to be unavailable to the self, it also leads to
attitudes that keep that which is envied unavailable. In addition to
disparaging it to make it unenviable and thus unworthy of pursuit,
or denying the desire for it so as not to feel envy, the person may
also make an assumption that others will have the same envious
attitude. This stands as another powerful deterrent against going
after what is actually wanted so intensely. Such an attitude certainly applies to power. The person reasons that "If *I* so hate and
envy the power and achievements of others, then others will hate
and envy mine." A fear of being envied develops. This reasoning
may lead to a lifelong scenario of self-sabotage. When success is
at hand, errors will be made that could well have been identified
and prevented. For example, one might "forget" to set the alarm
and thus oversleep, making it impossible to get to the all-
important interview for a new position entailing greater power
within an organization.

There is another kind of refusal of power that is motivated
by the wish to ward off envy, to present a picture of one's self as
unenviable. Dorothy and her husband have just purchased an
expensive new home. Dorothy is uncomfortable about having
more than her mother has, so when she tells her about the coming

move, she accentuates how much work it will be to take care of the house, how strapped for cash they will be and how they probably won't be able to take a vacation this year. By the time she has finished painting such a dismal picture to ensure that her mother (and others as well) will not envy her, she has taken all the pleasure out of the experience for herself. She has what she wants but she still feels unsatisfied. Indeed, as long as she must spoil whatever she has, and as long as she must diminish her own power or achievement or pleasure so as not to be the object of other people's envy, she will be unsatisfiable. And as long as she is unsatisfiable, she will feel deprived and she will herself be eaten up with envy of those who seem so happy with what they have. One can see how convoluted the thinking of individuals for whom envy is a central issue may become, and how they can get caught in a vicious circle from which there appears to be no escape. They continue to feel powerless and their self-esteem is similarly diminished. Dorothy takes to heart Lyly's aphorism that "The greatest harm you can do unto the envious, is to do well."[7] Although there are indeed envious people out there in the world, Dorothy's envy is the worst kind inasmuch as she sees it as universal; she suffers most from the projection and generalization of her own relentless and passionate envy.

The Next Step

At the other end of the rapprochement phase of development, the child strives actively to individuate further from the mother, to be defined as separate and unique in his or her own right. Since this developmental thrust is, in effect, a pushing away from her, it has overtones of aggression. The capacity of the mother to tolerate and encourage this progression, along with the amount of anger the child has stored up against her because of earlier disappoint-

---

[7]John Lyly, *Euphues* (1579).

ments, will affect the child's degree of comfort with the will and aggression that is needed to further its own development. Any undue guilt or anxiety that exists around these issues may lead to the inhibition of both will and aggression.

The next crisis in development arrives as the child's relationship with its parents becomes triangulated, and rivalry and jealousy enter the scene. Although rivalry and jealousy of a baby brother or sister may appear earlier, this situation is different. The new baby is only an intruder into the relationship with mother. It is not someone whose love the child also seeks. With the emergence of the true triangle, a new kind of conflict is experienced. The competitiveness that escalates with this triangulation and rivalry is another crisis point that may lead to a defensive refusal of power.

7

The Eternal Triangle

As the child differentiates and individuates more fully away from the early tie with the mother, becoming more and more of a person in his or her own right, mother and father also come to have a very different and distinct meaning and importance for the child. This was also true, in a way, earlier. From the earliest months the child is able to experience the difference between them, preferring mother at one time and father at another. But preoedipal relationships are dyadic, even though there are two separate dyads; one includes mother and child and the other includes father and child. The relationship with the father becomes particularly important, now enabling the child to move away from the symbiotic tie with the mother. A new island of safety makes it unnecessary to cling to the primary one. With growth and development widening the child's horizons, we see a three-way, or triadic relational system emerge.

With the emergence of the triangular conflict in the third year of life, a two-way competitiveness within the triangle generates new wishes, anxieties, and defenses. In Freud's terms, this is the stage when the Oedipus complex is activated. The child wants to be preferred by mother over father and by father over mother. Along with envy, the child now experiences jealousy of a rival whom he or she also loves, generating an uncomfortable ambivalence. Fear of punishment by the rival for these feelings develops. The conflict and anxiety generated in this situation may lead to psychological defenses that take the form of an eating disorder.

A young woman who still struggled with issues of power and powerlessness in that triangle, could only gain a sense of control by retreating to earlier battles around food with her mother. The conflict became focused within the earlier dyad rather than in the oedipal triangle. She reported, "My father was less available as I got older because of the power issues with Mom. She'd get in front of him and I couldn't get to him, and he allowed it. He relinquished his power and let her dominate. I couldn't fight for him. She was too powerful. I could only feel powerful around food. Later on if I felt sexual tension, I would eat to get rid of it." Thus eating became sexualized, and what was basically a conflict around power and sexuality was transformed into an eating disorder. One bodily impulse became a substitute for another that was experienced as more anxiety provoking.

The guilt and anxieties arising at this stage of development may be associated with healthy aggression, with going after what is wanted, and with sexual potency as well. This is the age when genital ascendency take the place of earlier foci of pleasure, such as those of sucking and swallowing. Hence, guilt and anxiety may lead to a refusal or turning away from power that significantly interferes with the achievement of adult goals both in work and in love. Behavioral patterns of self-sabotage, of diminishing the power of the self, may indicate that this dynamic is now in force.

At this point in development, the child's unique individuality becomes even more apparent (although it was there from the start). The world opens up to more complex learning experiences and more complex social interactions with entry into the peer society of nursery school or kindergarten. The strengths and vulnerabilities accumulated during the earliest years of life now shape the child's approach to and interactions with that world, including his or her experiences with and relationship to power.

Impotence and Playing It Safe

Barry presents himself to the world as powerless. He complains of being sexually impotent with women and of being pushed around by men. He describes the special closeness he had with his mother and how she fussed over his least sniffle. He enjoyed the attention, especially when she rubbed his chest with Vicks Vap-o-Rub. He continued this dependence even when he was in college and would drive the 150 miles home to take to his bed there when he was sick.

Barry recalls how he tried to look up his mother's dress when he was a child and how he would rummage around in her lingerie drawer, but denies that he had any conscious sexual fantasies about her. He did, however, have unrestrained images of fondling his aunt's breasts.

His father was relatively passive and did nothing to interfere with the mother's overprotection. He was fond of the boy and made attempts in Barry's earlier years to play with him and to interest him in activities away from home. But when Mother objected under the guise of concern that Barry might get hurt or sick, Father didn't fight her and Barry didn't protest, preferring the special and exciting closeness to mother. Father gave up trying when Barry was around 6 years old. Barry recalled with unexpected tears his father's disappointment when Barry said he didn't want to play catch. He had come to believe that he had been rejected by his father, but later came to understand that it had been the other way around. He had in fact rejected his father in preference to the specialness and closeness with his mother.

Barry also came to understand after some time in therapy, that he was forced to make himself sexually powerless in order to maintain the gratifying closeness with mother. This protected both of them from the dangers of incest. He learned to be close to her by being sick, by being ineffective and without power. This stance could be counted on to involve her with him. Paradoxically, he also covertly achieved the power to control mother through his apparent powerlessness. He got the wished for closeness and specialness, and could *control* the closeness and *defend* against the dangers of sexuality—all through taking on the demeanor of impotence. In psychoanalytic terminology this is called a *compromise formation*. It both achieves a forbidden wish and at the same time defends against the dangers of getting it.

Barry had also come to feel very guilty because of his competitive aggression with regard to his father where he seemed to come out the winner and the one closest to mother. Now, as an adult, any competitive strivings in the business world would lead to anxiety and guilt, and he would find a way to sabotage himself. He was a good tennis player, enjoying the intrinsic power that came with his strong forehand; however he usually lost the game, often hitting the ball into the net when he had a clear opening for a winning shot. His view of himself as a loser—in sex, at work and on the tennis court—led to a pervasive sense of shame and low self-esteem. He developed a fantasy life, however, in which he was very powerful and always won, but was concerned that he seemed to prefer his fantasy life to real relationships. Because he had developed such resentment and envy toward people who always seemed to win, who seemed able to pursue their goals unambivalently, he was afraid others would resent and envy him were he to do the same. He came to realize that he had seen his father's apparent rejection of him as punishment for his having pursued and won in the competition for his mother.

Barry is a person who rejects his own power and potency out of the anxiety and guilt associated with the oedipal stage of development, out of the competitive triangle that included him and his parents. He then has to find a way to counteract the shame associated with his defensive powerlessness, by means of constructing an illusory world for himself.

There are many stories like Barry's, of the renunciation of power in important areas of life because of conflicts unresolved from the days of the oedipal triangle.

Some men who are caught in Barry's dilemma can function adequately with a woman when the relationship is new and she is clearly not a member of the family. However, when they have been living together for some time, the woman takes on for him a feeling of familiarity similar to what he felt with his mother, and he can no longer function sexually. At this point he must find another woman who is more clearly "not-a-mother" in order to be potent. He seems always to need two women, one to live with and to provide emotional security, and another to be his sexual partner. This is not the same as the so-called madonna–whore split in which sexuality is deemed bad, but it is a mother-not-mother split. Resolution of the underlying fear of being powerful with mother will allow a healing of the split, while resolution of the underlying guilt about defeating father will enable a successful pursuit of goals. In order to do this, the man must give up the pleasure of being special to mother, and end his denial of the reality of a sexual bond between mother and father. He will have to find healthier and more mature roads to pride and power.

When toddlers enter the wider world of childhood, they do so with an already existing relationship to their own power and to that of others. Their negotiation of the developmental tasks of childhood may be facilitated or restricted depending on this pre-existing stance, and new power issues will emerge in the light of old ones.

8

Childhood

During the school years, there is a rapid unfolding of many innate potentials as the child develops in size, strength, and coordination, as the ability to think becomes more and more complex, with the emergence of the capacity for abstract ideas. One 6-year-old philosopher asked his mother, "How do we know that God is not dreaming us, and that when He wakes up is when we die?"

Talents also emerge, from the prodigious, as with a 6-year-old Mozart, to the more mundane abilities of the child whose finger-paintings are taped to the refrigerator door. Interests begin to jell and hobbies reflect those interests.

This rapid expansion of the child's personality is particularly relevant to intrinsic power, to a deep sense of one's ability to be in the world as a person of worth to others and to himself as well. When these unfolding potentialities are hampered because of pre-existing insecurities that develop from troubled relationships with important figures at home, the development of a sense of intrinsic power is thwarted as well.

In the competitive atmosphere of the classroom and the schoolyard, power takes on a different kind of significance. Power hierarchies develop along many lines and range from class leader to playground bully. The child's ability to be in this world without undue anxiety, without having either to retreat in fear, or to develop a defensive "no one can push me around" attitude, will be affected by his relation to his own intrinsic power as well as to the power of others, and to that degree to which he may attribute power to other children that must then cause him concern.

Childhood and Competence

Erik Erikson (1950) describes the childhood years as a time to develop "industry," a time to adjust oneself to the inorganic laws of the world of tools. It is a time to learn to be part of a productive situation. "His ego boundaries include his tools and skills . . . [he learns] the pleasure of work completion by steady attention and persevering diligence" (p. 227).

In power terms, childhood is a time to widen the experience of intrinsic power. Powers of the physical self develop through exertion of strength, speed, coordination, skill, and toleration of physical discomfort. In the classroom, the intrinsic power of the intellect is similarly exercised. Erikson tells us that if this developmental thrust is inhibited because of preexisting unresolved developmental conflicts within the family, the child will develop a sense of inferiority.

Only when there is a secure sense of the "I am," and a belief that the determination of the "I will" is supported by important authority figures, can the "I can" be allowed to encompass ever-widening parameters in the world beyond the family.

The child who is anxiously focused on whether or not the teacher likes him or her, or who takes a negative stance toward the teacher in a kind of perversion of the need for power and control, will be unable to use the teacher as a resource—as someone to learn from, someone to enable the "I can." The interpersonal power struggle takes precedence over becoming knowledgeable and competent. Acknowledging that the teacher is of value and has something to give may evoke envy and a need to spoil him or her. And just as some children need to defeat the teacher, so some people who seek psychotherapy need to defeat the therapist. They cannot use the therapist as a resource in adulthood for the same reasons they may have been unable to use their teachers as a resource during childhood. The power per se of the teacher's authority may be hated and envied, as that of the parents may be; and an overthrow of that power, by rendering the teacher powerless, may be all that matters.

The child who competitively seeks to be best loved by the teacher and who sets up peers as either sibling or oedipal rivals will be unable to explore new ways of competence in the peer world. Other children will react negatively to the attitude of superiority that comes to that child by virtue of being special to the powerful authority figure. They will also react negatively to that child's obvious need to defeat them, to make them less-than. Social rejection and hostility then further cut the child off from the peer world as a place to widen intrinsic power through the practice and learning of new skills.

The child who must win in order not to be humiliated, or who withdraws from the contest because of fear of being humiliated, or because of anxiety and guilt about winning, will not develop the physical skills that will enhance his or her sense of intrinsic power. For these children it is not how you play the game that matters; it is whether you win or lose. Once again, these attitudes alienate other children and thus cut off avenues of growth.

Children act out with their peers the needs they have for power and control. The playground bully turns the tables, trying to undo the shame and powerlessness of his being bullied at home. Adults who got stuck on the power issues of the earlier years, and who were therefore unable to develop a real and valid sense of their own competence in childhood, often present themselves as "unable." This inability can refer to such matters as taking care of bills, managing personal business matters in general, or knowing what to do and how to do it in the adult world of travel and commerce. In addition to developing the need, described earlier, to be incompetent within a family relational system, some truly do not develop the skills for living even though they are fully equipped intellectually to do so. Their failure to develop intrinsic power leaves them feeling dependent on, or fearful of, the power of others, with all of the interpersonal problems that come with the dynamics of this situation.

The childhood years are characterized as the "latency period" in psychoanalytic theory, a time during which interpersonal strivings take a backseat to development of other facets of the personality. Supposedly the sexuality of the oedipal period becomes quiescent, to surface again with the advent of puberty. Precocious romantic involvements with girlfriends or boyfriends during the childhood years suggest anxiety at being separated from parents and out in the world without a special, emotionally intense relationship. These overinvolvements often get in the way of the further unfolding of intrinsic power, of developing what Erikson refers to as "industry."

In Erikson's terms, a good relation to "the world of skills and tools" enables the child to move on to the developmental tasks of adolescence. With puberty and the capacity for adult forms of sexuality, power once again takes on greater *interpersonal* significance. And with the task of separating from parents in a more far-reaching way, one's power in regard to parents surfaces again as an issue.

9

I Am, I Can, and I Will

In his sensitive short story, "I Don't Need You Anymore," Arthur Miller writes of a little boy who angrily spits out these words at his mother in his attempt to extricate himself from the web of her overprotection. He wants desperately to be one of the men:

> And suddenly he remembered: "I don't need you any more!" His own words came back, shrill and red with fury. Why was that so terrible? He didn't need her anymore. He could tie his laces now, he could walk forever without getting tired. . . . She didn't want him, why did he have to pretend he wanted her? The horror in it escaped him. Still, it probably was horrible anyway, only he didn't understand why. . . . How fine it would be to sink into the ocean now, he thought. How she would plead with his dead, shut-eyed face to say something.

Mr. Miller conveys beautifully the struggle for selfhood and for manhood in this young boy-child, and shows how, in anger at his mother's frustration of his wish to be separate and autonomous, he denies to her and to himself his need and love for her.

Three aspects of intrinsic power are related to the child's ability to move away from the mother: *Existence,* and later, *identity,* which is expressed by the words, "I am"; *mastery,* which is expressed by the words, "I can"; and *intentionality,* which is expressed by the words, "I will."

74

I Am

Cogito, ergo sum: I think, therefore I am. More than 300 years ago, René Descartes in his "Discourse on Method" understood that this inborn capacity of the human organism, this biological foundation of intrinsic power, was the key to his sense of self and existence. He believed it was possible to doubt everything else, but not one's own existence. As soon as one tries to doubt one's existence, it is clear that one must exist as the doubter. You cannot doubt that you are doubting.

One woman told me how, "There was an issue of loyalty to mother. You had to be loyal in your thinking and think the way she did, so you just didn't think. If you insisted on your view, it would be like killing her, stealing her power, annihilating her adulthood. Just thinking was destructive." This woman had had to give up that very basic intrinsic power of which Descartes spoke, her capacity to think, so as not to steal her mother's power and not thereby destroy her. When we consider Descartes's words, we realize how devastating to one's identity and very existence the renunciation of this intrinsic power can be.

Men and women sometimes go to a psychotherapist because they feel they do not exist; they feel they are not real, and they are afraid to look within for fear there will be nothing there. Descartes would say that the ability to think and express those ideas was proof in itself that the person does indeed exist. For who *is* describing these troublesome feelings by means of coherent speech with a well-ordered syntax?

The newborn infant cannot walk or talk or feed itself or control its bowels. But its brain is busy at work sorting out patterns and sensations which, after a time, will come to be invested with meaning; and with the construction of meaning the person will have developed a mind. Just as the ability to think is the taproot of existence, of the sense of "I am," it is also the taproot of intrinsic power. Nothing is more devastating to the developing child than to have its ability to think—and to think clearly—

undercut by parents who, for their own reasons, need to have absolute power not only over what is said, but over what is thought and believed in the family.

The most simple, yet elegant, statement of intrinsic power is, "I am. I exist. I go on." It is an affirmation of one's existence as a unique being. It is a statement that carries with it a recognition of one's separateness from mother, of one's final individuation out of the earlier symbiotic union and its fused image of self and object. This developmental stride may feel destructive to the child insofar as it is a pushing away from the mother, a rejection of union with her, and thus, in effect, a rejection of her.

The ability and willingness of the mother to not only allow but also *support* the child's statement of separateness from her will set the stage for the child's ability to sustain the anxieties and conflicts of forward development without undue anxiety or depression. There will be anxiety if the child feels that development must proceed without the mother because she withdraws her emotional support; and there will be depression if the child feels a profound loss of her and of her love. But the statement of separateness is essential if the child is to develop a sense of identity, and of the intrinsic power of the *I am*.

The push away from mother requires not only the will or intention to do it, but the freedom to use a certain amount of aggression in the service of that individuation. It involves saying no to her, thereby challenging her power and control. It may make her sad, as she recognizes that she is losing "her baby." If she is too sad and the child becomes aware of her feelings, he or she will feel that the mother has been hurt or damaged by the intrinsic power, will, and aggression of the self. The power of the self will be experienced as too great and too dangerous. It may have to be inhibited, or completely repressed, with a renunciation of both identity and intrinsic power. The resulting frustration of the healthy wish to individuate, and the loss of all that individuation implies, leads to a build-up of resentment and anger, which then adds to the potential danger of any kind of power that is achieved. The wish to kill the mother, to get her out of the way, may even be conscious, which further frightens the small child who is also very dependent on his primary caretaker, and which makes him feel enormously guilty. A vicious cycle of anxiety and guilt and the resultant self-inhibiting defenses, which lead to a refusal to be powerful in any way, is set in motion. Arthur Miller's character had a fantasy of suicide in reaction to his guilt and frustration, and the wish to hurt his mother was clearly embedded in that fantasy. He would make her feel as terrible because he killed himself as he felt at his symbolic killing of her. The aggression he needed in order to establish both his identity and his intrinsic power was imploded, directed inward against himself.

The False Self

If the child feels unsupported in his or her attempts to become separate from the mother, he or she may find a way to relate to her—and to others later in life—that keeps any manifestation of will or aggression securely in check (and with it, any sense of power). The false self is an identity that is based upon reactions to the other person, a self that takes its cue from that person. The false self both enables a connection to the other, and protects the true self from the other. The false self is a responder but never an initiator: One can react through the false self by complying *with,* by struggling *against,* by performing *for,* by warding *off,* or by complaining *about.* The false self is a prepositional self and does not own the pronoun "I." Any experience of the intrinsic power of the "I am" must be kept secret and hidden or expressed in disguised forms. Only in the context of a relationship in which the individual feels safe and accepted can the *I am* be openly stated, even if that entails conflict with the other. Sometimes the "I am" is experienced only in a secret fantasy life in which there is an exaggerated image of an independent all-powerful self that needs nothing from anyone. This can exist side-by-side with a frightened, cut-off, helpless self. Because the person's intrinsic power has thus been blocked in its development, the true self feels powerless and helpless. Carried to the extreme, the annihilation of the *I am* leads to a state of terror, of panic at non-being, of feeling oneself at the mercy of shapeless emotions that cannot be articulated.

In therapy, the coexistence of the different selves—the false self, the true frightened self, and the defensive and compensatory grandiose self—is explored with the aim of integrating these split selves into a single unified, realistic, and secure self whose intrinsic power is freed up to be expressed in work, in creativity, and in interpersonal relationships.

I Can

The sense of mastery, of competence, and of effectiveness, is central to intrinsic power. "See what I can do!" is the exclamation of the child feeling the pride of that power. From feeding himself, to dressing himself, to putting a puzzle together, to riding a bike with no hands, the world of the "I can" expands and widens with experience and learning. It is an avenue of growth that can be lifelong, although it is most central during the years of childhood when it begins with steps toward individuation. That avenue of intrinsic power may be blocked early on, however.

A particularly malignant manifestation of false-self identity is that which develops when, as a child, the individual had to be the container of aspects of the mother or father that the parent disowned in herself or himself. One of the most frequently disowned aspects of the self is a sense of powerlessness, inadequacy, and shame. A baby or small child is a natural to take on that role. After all, it is realistically smaller and less powerful than its parents. When the mother *keeps on relating* to the child as if he or she were helpless and inadequate and takes for herself the role of the adequate helper, the only one who knows what to do, the child may come to believe this reflection of himself and come to feel he or she *is* that powerless, inadequate creature. Increasingly cut off from any inner definition of the self and from access to the intrinsic power of the *I am,* the child is also cut off from the intrinsic power of the *I can.* It knows only the impotence of a stance of "I cannot."

In such a situation, any statement of competence, of "I can do it myself!" stands as a refusal to collude with the parent's need to hold onto an all-powerful and perfect self-image, and may be experienced by this parent as an attack. Indeed it is an attack on the parent's defensive illusions about his or her self. Thus there is an element of aggression perceived in such a refusal. Once again guilt at hurting the parent can evoke a backing-down from the *I can*—in effect, a refusal by the child to own the intrinsic power of the self. The result is not only a sense of being powerless, but also feelings of shame or humiliation. Whereas feelings of existence go with the *I am,* feelings of self-esteem go with the *I can.* In the absence of the first, the individual is likely to feel annihilation anxiety. In the absence of the second, he or she is likely to feel shame.

I Will

When there is an "I" that exists, and a self that can, conscious expressions of will—of *intentionality*—come to the fore. Although intentionality as a built-in behavior is there from the start, a *consciously articulated* intention requires a sense of existence and of the capacity for mastery. The healthy development of will is inhibited when the other aspects of intrinsic power have not developed. When this happens, the will may continue to be manifest, but in self- or other-destructive ways wherein it becomes dedicated to the expression of rage or despair.

It is at this stage of development, when consciously articulated intention becomes more prominent, that the power struggles with parents take on a more serious tone. They may take place at first around such issues as eating or sleeping or toileting;

later, the child's developing goals and interests require access to will if they are to be pursued.

The power struggle can develop anywhere along the developmental continuum, and is more likely to do so if parents act out their own power needs. When, and around which issues, their power needs surface will depend upon their own developmental history. The acting out of power needs by a parent is very different from the expression of appropriate parental authority consistent with the child's age and requirements. When the child has not yet developed internal controls, parents have to supply them. If they do not, the child may become anxious about the consequent lack of structure and predictability. Sometimes, when parents do not provide this structure, the child may feel the power vacuum and move to fill it himself or herself. Such a child may become rigidly controlling in order to avoid the anxiety of feeling out of control.

The development of a child's will may go off course with parents who make extreme demands for performance or achievement, and with those who take away the child's opportunity to make the kinds of decisions that are an expression of will. In these instances, all that is left to enable a child to experience its own power is the statement "I will not." This kind of oppositionalism to parental demands may, in the short or long run, prove to be destructive to the individual. He or she may be prevented from following any real intentionality because it will feel like submission to parental power. There may be a sabotage of the individual's own goals and abilities in the process. Saying no becomes important not only to define one's self as separate, and to have a sense of "I am"; saying no becomes important to preserve an illusion of will, and with it, of intrinsic power.

Will may also be subjected to repression and inhibition when it is suffused with anger and is experienced as an act *against* the other. In one example, a young man was struggling to find not only his sense of who he was, his identity, but to re-find the intrinsic power that seemed to have gotten lost earlier in his life. He said, "I have to use my strength against my parents to be a man, to make an independent decision. When I make a decision, they lose control of my life. It shows I'm not an outgrowth of them. Sometimes all this makes me feel guilty. When I expressed my own feelings as a child, I was put down. Now a war has to be fought to get my feelings out. I'm impressed with some of the things I get done. My power blows me away. The more powerless I feel, the more excited I become when I *do* feel powerful."

Some small children may at times actually feel their sense of *I am* and *I will* to be endangered by a loving and empathic mother. The warmth and closeness may be experienced as a temptation to regress that has to be resisted. These children may be negativistic and even belligerent at such times. This, of course, is puzzling and frustrating for parents. They may, in turn, react angrily, which is not at all what the child really wants. He or she may then feel sad or even a little depressed. The child vascillates between warm, loving behavior, and tantrums or other forms of controlling behavior. The wish to feel powerful and proud takes precedence over love at these times.

If parents can understand such behavior as a manifestation of the need to feel strong and thus unafraid, they can pay special attention to enabling and supporting the child's developing intrinsic powers, particular in the areas of the *I can*. This does not mean that they must submit to the child's attempts to control them. If they do, the child may become frightened at his or her power to overcome that of the parents, for it is in that benevolent power that his or her security lies. Firmness in the appropriate setting of limits is a benevolent use of power, inasmuch as it protects the child from its out-of-control aggression.

Some "self psychologists" will insist that this behavior is a manifestation of parental failures in empathy. They do not agree that aggression and the conflict between loving and aggressive impulses are intrinsic to normal, healthy development; or that as much as the child wishes at times to be lovingly connected to the parents, he or she also wants to push against them and away from them at other times in the interest of separateness and individuality, as well as feelings of power and pride.

10

*Adolescence:
Getting It Together*

Toward the end of childhood and with entry into adolescence, new factors come to the fore—sexuality in both boys and girls, and in boys, a heightened press of aggression resulting from the production of testosterone. Unlike a hobby that can be pursued in social isolation, these emerging energies entail a coming to terms with the interpersonal world to a greater and greater degree. Any power conflicts that developed with parents are likely to affect these new relationships as the young person struggles to escape from the inherent powerlessness of being small.

Furthermore, as the young person also struggles out of dependency, there may be a need to create illusions of greater power within the self, to develop forms of defensive or compensatory power to make up for the felt vulnerability and powerlessness of the dependent position.

Power struggles between adolescent and parents may be reminiscent of those of the 2-year-old, with analogous thrusts toward increasing autonomy. In truth, if one is to become a grown-up in a world of grown-ups, sooner or later there must be an "overthrow" of parental authority, with a resultant change in the locus of security, direction, decision-making, and the taking of responsibility. This "overthrow" is not necessarily rebellious in nature but a manifestation of maturing inner regulators, guides, principles, and values, some of which have been learned from parental figures. These inner regulators are now felt as an aspect of one's self, rather than as compliance with an external authority.

Anxiety and guilt about taking this necessary developmental step may be one factor in an individual's refusal of power in adult life.

The Developmental Tasks

The developmental tasks of adolescence all have a power dimension. The boy's or girl's relationship to power—to the intrinsic power of the self, the *I am* and the *I can* and the *I will,* versus a need for defensive or compensatory power; and to his or her characteristic role in the power balance within the family—will affect how he or she negotiates these tasks.

Assimilation of the new pubescent body, the physiological changes, and the upsurge of sexual desires have to be achieved and then integrated into the sense of an ongoing self, the sense of "this is still me." In particular, the power of the *I am* is critical if this is to take place. Without that core solidity, the new appearance and the new feelings can be fragmenting or disorganizing. Anxiety, uncertainty as to identity, and fear of losing control may be overwhelming. The eating disorders often develop at this juncture with an attempt to gain omnipotent control over the body, its form and its impulses. This defensive illusion of power counteracts the terror of helplessness against forces over which one has no control. The new helplessness re-evokes earlier terrors of helplessness against controlling and intrusive parents.

Another task is the establishment of heterosexual relationships, the ability to relate to members of the opposite sex. In childhood there was a tendency to group with members of the same sex, with the shared goals of developing skills and interests and a sense of one's self as a boy or a girl through peer relating. Now the pull is in the other direction, to establish a sense of one's self as male or female through the eyes of the opposite sex, to have that maleness or femaleness affirmed through sexuality rather than through skills and interests. Since boyfriends or girlfriends can take on the power to affirm the self, to make the self feel not only attractive but lovable, parental power may be attributed to such a friend—making the self especially vulnerable and open to feelings of powerlessness and shame once again with regard to a parental figure. The more solid the sense of intrinsic power, the less likely the young person is to suffer these agonies and to settle once again into a dependent and powerless position.

Still another developmental task of adolescence is the development of a philosophy of life. This will include not only a sense of what is right and what is wrong, but also the values, the goals, and the standards by which one wants to live. If these standards are met, the person feels good about himself or herself. Essentially, in psychoanalytic terms, this marks the firming up of the superego, that part of the personality that is comprised of the conscience and the "ego ideal." This developmental task entails the taking into the self of power that once lay with the parents. In one way, parental authority must be overthrown and that guiding authority must come to reside within the self.

To the extent that the young person feels good about parental authority and admires the parents, this task may be relatively unconflicted. Much of what one's parents have espoused is taken on truly as one's own, although other models and heroes will have made alterations in the picture of what the young person wants for himself or herself. When parental power and authority have been experienced as benevolent and as a source of security and self-esteem, it is a power to be emulated, not one to be envied, hated, and overthrown. When there have been earlier power struggles, with parents unable to gradually relinquish control and enable the child to take on more and more responsibility for choices and actions, the boy or girl may have come to feel the necessity to completely overthrow parental authority. This may lead to a kind of oppositionalism, a refusal to identify with parental values and standards. But this compulsory oppositionalism, with its underlying wish to define the self, gets in the way of doing just that. It is more important for such a child to *not* be like the mother or *not* be like the father. A negative identity is no identity at all. Furthermore, hatred of parental power produces conflict in the young person with respect to having power of his or her own. Who wants to be like the abusive father or controlling mother! To be a self that one can love and feel good about, one has to be unlike the unacceptable model; and this may entail a refusal of power to enable one to live up to a picture of the self that can be cherished. Unfortunately, this deliberate refusal of power, because of its negative connotations, may lead the individual to feel powerless in the world, a situation that paradoxically acts *against* the self-esteem that the refusal of power first set out to ensure.

Nietzsche wrote in *The Will to Power* that "Virtues are as dangerous as vices, insofar as they are allowed to rule over one as authorities and laws coming from outside, and not as qualities one develops oneself." And, he adds, these inner qualities should be "the determining factors of precisely *our* existence and growth, which we recognize and acknowledge independently of the question [of] whether others grow with us with the help of the same or of different principles" (pp. 96–97). This inner source of guidance, that is neither in compliant conformity with authority figures nor in opposition to them, becomes a significant aspect of intrinsic power.

However, if parents have a strong need to maintain their power in the power balance and to keep their son or daughter in the more powerless and diminished position, it may seem to the young person that the only way to get adult power is to overthrow the authority of the parents. In effect, the parents have to be deposed; and if they feel shamed or diminished by this change in the balance of power, the young person will have to deal with the guilt of having somehow hurt the parents, or with the anxiety of feeling one has destroyed them and left oneself alone in the world.

Still another developmental task of adolescence is the definition of life goals, of aims that will eventually integrate the knowledge, abilities, skills, and interests that began to develop in the childhood years. As they become more fully elaborated they too are part of the reservoir of intrinsic power that includes not only the *I am,* but also the *I can* and the *I will.* The use of these aspects of intrinsic power toward the achievement of one's own goals and aims, along with comfort in the use of the aggression necessary to their pursuit, will enable the boy or girl to face this task without undue anxiety or guilt.

Perhaps the most troublesome task of adolescence is the further move toward independence and separateness from parents. In this task, adolescence recapitulates the task of the rapprochement stage of development that started in the second year of life. Like the earlier challenge, this too requires the support of the parents if it is to be met without anxiety, guilt, or the depression of loss. It is important for the child to know that the overthrow of parental authority by the very act of becoming one's own authority, and the parents' loss of identity *as parents*—that may result from one's leaving behind one's identity *as child*—have neither destroyed nor alienated the parents; and to know that the parents can still be counted on to "be there," that their love has not been withdrawn. No degree of intrinsic power will be likely to make the continuation of that love and concern irrelevant to the grown son or daughter.

With a secure sense of self and of one's intrinsic power, it is not as frightening to take independent action and to bear responsibility for it. However, if there are strong undercurrents of feelings of powerlessness and inadequacy, the young person may possibly bolster himself or herself with the illusory power of being part of a gang that makes a point of showing *its* power in antisocial or even criminal ways. Compensatory power and pride may be sought through acceptable social channels, such as popularity among one's peers and success in school politics. But when the pursuit of goals has as its main function the overcoming of feelings of shame and powerlessness, achievement of these goals effects only a cosmetic change and often cannot be integrated to effect any real change in the sense of intrinsic power.

Erikson (1950) notes that the supraordinate task of integrating all of these adolescent tasks and changes leads to a sense of what he calls "ego identity." He defines this as "the accrued confidence that the inner sameness and continuity are matched by the sameness and continuity of one's meaning for others. . . ." (p. 228).

He contrasts the achievement of ego identity with "role diffusion," associating this state both with doubt as to one's sexual identity, and with the inability to settle on an occupational identity. Erikson describes some of the adolescent's defenses against the disturbing experience of role diffusion, defenses such as temporarily overidentifying with heroes or with cliques and crowds. He also cites falling in love and using the love object as a mirror through which a reflection of the self helps to clarify and define who that self is. "This is why many a youth would rather converse, and settle matters of mutual identification, than embrace," he tells us (p. 228). He adds his observation that "puberty rites and confirmations help to integrate and to affirm the new identity."

If we reread Erikson, keeping in mind questions concerning power—intrinsic power, attributed power, and defensive or compensatory power—we can see how the power dimension helps to shape the process as Erikson describes it.

By the end of adolescence, certain identifications with both the mother and the father become consolidated. These identifications are a culmination of the many ways in which the child internalizes aspects of both parents and makes these part of the self from the earliest years onward. This process is an integral part of the structuring of the self which takes place in the interpersonal matrix.

Sometimes an individual is conflicted about these identifications, especially when power is involved. A boy who sees his mother as the powerful parent and his father as the weak one is caught in a dilemma: If he is to be male like his father, he will also be weak; if he is strong like his mother, this identification endangers his sense of maleness.

On the other hand, girls who see their mothers as weak may associate weakness with femininity and are thus conflicted about their own gender. How can they be strong without being masculine?

If the powerful parent uses his or her power to hurt the child, either physically or emotionally, that power comes to be hated and feared. The child may have to reject having power in order to be the kind of person he or she wants to be. Yet to be this desired self may mean being weak, powerless, and shamed.

The final outcome of the identification process is strongly influenced by the balance of power within the family, and by the child's perception of power as male or female, benevolent or malevolent. The individual's relationship to his or her own power is affected by these identifications and the degree to which they are conflicted or conflict-free. Ultimately, the way out of the dilemma is the realization that to be *like* the parent is not the same as *being* the parent, and that one can take power and make of it whatever one chooses.

The New Forces

Freud observed the prominent roles that sex and aggression played in the psychologies of the people he studied and worked with. He postulated that these "instincts" guided development, and thus they became the "organizing principle" for his theories. Sexuality was said to usually follow a predictable course of development, and to have an organizing function in that development. Others did not agree that these instincts were the prime determinants of behavior, and pointed out how their form and expression seemed to be determined by the interpersonal context within which they emerged. From this point of view, the interpersonal situation and the resulting inner images of self and other (*object relations*) became the organizing principle. From Freud's perspective, the upsurge of sexuality and aggression that come with biological maturation strongly influences the course of adolescent development. From the object relations or interpersonal perspective, the characteristic manner in which the individual relates to others—and this includes issues of power—will determine the form, relative manageability, and expression of sexuality and aggression in adolescence and beyond. It is likely that these biologically innate behaviors, and the relational context within which they are shaped and become expressed, affect one another in a mutual and reciprocal manner. Just as there is a power dimension to all human relationships, there is likely to be a power aspect to sexual and aggressive behaviors. The need for power either as defense or compensation, or the refusal to be powerful out of anxiety or guilt, will affect both the manner in which sexuality becomes integrated into one's life, and the ability to use the aggression necessary for the pursuit of one's goals. The integration of these two forces constitutes one of the major tasks of adolescence.

The Power of Sex

Sex as a form of power is discovered by the adolescent who is suddenly pursued because of his or her personal attractiveness or because of prominent sexual features, such as the large breasts of an early-maturing pubescent girl. He or she may have felt powerless with regard to parents, unable to have an impact, unable to be sure of parental availability or support. The power of parents to give or withhold was painfully obvious because it was not always used in a benevolent fashion. But now the tables are turned. There is a new form of power with the potential to control others. The stronger the need to control an emotionally important other, the more likely it is that sex will be dedicated to this purpose. The healthy integration of sexuality as an aspect of intrinsic power is undermined. Instead of being part of the self, sex becomes a weapon used by the self to control others.

Becoming an Adult in an Adult World

Having built up and built in a strong sense of the intrinsic power of the *I am,* the *I can,* and the *I will* at each step along the developmental continuum—in a manner appropriate for each stage and its level of mental, social, and physical maturity—the individual can move forward, feeling himself or herself to be an adult in the adult world. The full assimilation of the developmental changes does not take place all at once, but may be a gradual process taking several years to accomplish. Many people in the transitional decade of the twenties feel themselves to have one foot in the adult world and the other still lagging behind in the psychological world of the child. There is often a sense of relief at turning thirty, as an objective indication that one is essentially over the hump, that one now has to be taken seriously, that one is no longer a bright and precocious child to be patted condescendingly on the head. Although there is gratification and pleasure in being the bright and special child, the promising protegé, this carries with it a relative powerlessness and potential for shame vis-à-vis the world of grown-ups. To claim the full power of adult status, a power based on the security of intrinsic power, one gives up the more immature gratifications. Most people would say that the trade-off is worthwhile.

Part III

Psychopathology
of Power

11

*The Generational
Transmission
of Powerlessness*

If we begin with a young mother who feels deeply inadequate, inferior, and powerless, the stage is set for the handing down of this burden to the next generation. When she has a baby, it clearly *is* powerless. It can't tie its own shoes, so by adult standards it is also inadequate (although it may be perfectly adequate for its age). As she cares for the child, our young mother begins to experience a new kind of adequacy and power. The disparity between them actually makes her feel better. Here is a creature far worse off than she is. Her self-esteem soon becomes tied to her function *as a mother,* to the role itself. She is the mother who always knows best, who knows what to do and how to do it, who knows what is right, what is good, and what is of value in this world. She becomes locked into this stance by way of her child; and if her self-esteem is to survive, she must keep the child eternally in this position. In effect, she has put her powerlessness and shame into this child who now functions as a container for them. The child develops a false self-identity that is consolidated around this image, and it will be part of his or her experience as a person.

But the story is not complete. She not only has to get rid of her inadequacy, but must also keep up a compensatory over-adequacy, superiority, omnipotence, and perfection. If her child's mission in life is to sustain and maintain the mother's self-esteem, he or she has to do this as well for her. She has to be able to be proud of him or of her. "My son, the doctor!" is the way this is often caricatured in the case of a male child. After all, he is an extension of her, so as much as she needs him to be powerless and inadequate, she also needs him to be exactly the opposite. He becomes the container of her projected grandiosity and thus now has *two* false self-identities that are consolidated around the mother's projections. One is powerless, impotent in life, and ridden with shame. The other is powerful and prideful, to the point of grandiosity. Because of the need for these compensatory feelings, he is usually unrealistic about what he can and cannot do, setting himself up for real failure in the outside world.

Alongside these two false selves, his true self, whoever that might be, is thwarted in its development; there is both rage at the situation, at the feeling of being utterly controlled by the mother, and there is depression at the apparent hopelessness of the dilemma. He is in a classical "double-bind" situation in which he must obey two totally contradictory injunctions and, at the same time, is barred from acknowledging or confronting the contradiction. Slipp (1984) points out how the child receives two messages: "Succeed for me but fail for me." Along with the mission of justifying his mother's pride goes another level of power, the illusory omnipotence of having total control over his mother's self-esteem. This power is very frightening, as it seems to him that he has the power to save or to destroy her. He may introduce another kind of impotence, a defensive powerlessness, that has as its aim both the preservation of the needed and ambivalently loved mother, and the protection of her from his potentially destructive fury at the incapacitating power she has over him.

The entire scenario may be replayed with the next generation, as he repeats the process either with his wife or with one of his own children.

This way of being and way of relating to others becomes built into the individual's "character structure." It is also played out with friends or acquaintances, as well as with husbands, wives, or children. This individual often is, in reality, very competent, and may tend toward work situations in which one is required to "take charge." His or her success in this setting reinforces the defensive superadequacy. Individuals with this character defense are likely to get into conflict with others who will not, consciously or unconsciously, go along with the maintenance of their posture of superadequacy—of omnipotence and perfection. These conflicts may arise in both work and personal situations. Any threat to these defenses evokes hostility, and a feeling that one is being challenged. There may even be a paranoid flavor to the reactions insofar as any threat to the defense is experienced as dangerous for the hidden powerless self.

A young woman had held a special position in the family as her father's shining star. This continued into her adult life. He could not tolerate her having any independent achievement, and if she reported something of which she was proud, he would react with stony silence and go on as though she had not said anything. She sabotaged her own promising career and became the perennial woman behind the powerful man, getting her own pride and sense of power by proxy through his adoration of her. She too had received the message "Succeed for me but fail for me," although the failure was hidden behind what appeared on the surface to be success in her position of "right hand" to the man. Her failure was in regard to the development of her own intrinsic talents. It was only by giving up the wish to be adored by the idealized father figure, and the gratification of being so adored—and then by mourning the loss of her only positive interaction with her father—that she was able to go on to develop her intrinsic power creatively and effectively.

12

The Eroticizing of Power

Henry Kissinger observed that power is the ultimate aphro-disiac. Liz Smith, the gossip columnist, presented a variation on the theme, saying that money is the ultimate aphrodisiac. What-ever the symbol for power, it clearly turns people on.

A successful woman executive noted that "to be sexually attracted I have to see a man as powerful—more powerful than me. It's what excites me. I'm not attracted to the nice guy who loves me."

Another woman recalled the sudden loss of sexual feelings toward her father when she realized he was powerless to protect her in a dangerous situation at her high school.

Still another could not understand why she needed fantasies of being humiliated in order to feel "turned on."

A man spoke of the domination–submission games he played out with his homosexual partners. He emphasized that there was no wish to hurt or to be hurt; that what was exciting was the sense of power, not the act of aggression. Wondering how this would apply to the submissive partner, he concluded that in the act of submis-sion, he shared in the excitement of the other person's power, which he felt unable to experience within himself. This recalls how the infant participates in its mother's power; and how some women who have not developed and integrated their own intrinsic power achieve a sense of power, pride, and prestige through their husbands.

Stoller (1975) characterizes the perversions as "the erotic form of hatred." The experience of power in the expression of that hatred plays a major part in its potential for excitement. Eroticism and power become inextricably woven together. We must look to the nature of an individual's most intensely, emotionally significant interpersonal relationships in the earliest years of life to understand the evolution of his or her eroticism. The variety of its expressions will reflect the variety of kinds of relationships that exist between parents and their children.

Human development can be viewed from a number of different perspectives. In this book, the perspective is the locus, nature, and experience of power. In *Being and Loving,* the perspective is identity and the capacity for intimacy. Another perspective is what is called, in psychoanalytic theory, *psychosexual stages.* With this approach, the development of eroticism becomes the "organizing principle."

This term refers to the way we order and organize our data, and the perspective from which we view the resultant observations. A pile of wooden blocks of various colors, sizes, and shapes can be sorted according to color, according to shape, or according to size. Each sorting has a different organizing principle, and the resulting piles may look quite different from one another depending upon which organizing principle was used. We always begin with the same pile of blocks, but each sorting has its own inherent "truth."

Different theories of human development often start with the same "pile of blocks," with the same observations of human behavior. However, they organize the data according to different principles. One may be no more true than another; what is at issue is the immediate usefulness of a given sorting. The concept of psychosexual stages is especially useful in our attempt to understand how power may become eroticized.

The first of the psychosexual stages is the *oral* stage, which is divided into sucking and biting. A child can be comforted with a bottle or by sucking its thumb. Later tension may be reduced by nail-biting. As adults, most of us are aware of the erotic pleasure associated with kissing. The persistence of oral pleasure is particularly evident in such activities as eating, drinking, and smoking.

The second stage is referred to as the *anal* stage at which time the child's interest shifts to the sensitive areas of the body associated with elimination. The third and final stage is the *genital* one. At this time the sexual organs and the feelings experienced with regard to them take on the greatest importance, and are most typically the focus of excitement and interest throughout life, although not exclusively.

As the capacity for genital eroticism gains in intensity in the second year of life, and into the third year, it will attach itself to the relationship that is most salient for the child at the time of its ascendency. That relationship will provide the vehicle for its expression, and sexuality thus becomes integrated within this interpersonal relationship. When sexuality is split off from the relationship, it may be to avoid felt dangers of their coming together. If this relationship is one that is characterized by tenderness and affection, tenderness and affection will become eroticized. If, on the other hand, this relationship is characterized by sadism and humiliation, by the abusive use of power, then this is what will become eroticized. The relationship and sexuality, both being highly charged for the child, are drawn together like the positive and negative poles of two magnets. Clinical research (Wolfson 1987), supports the view that both heterosexuality and homosexuality are "powerfully influenced by and can originate in motivational systems other than the erotic—like power and dependency strivings" (p. 171).

Eroticized cruelties are acted out and made real in some of the perversions. If parents have been emotionally unavailable and the child has turned to objects for comfort, such an object can become the focus of eroticism, achieving the status of a fetish. This can also come about in situations where objects are felt to be safer than the people with whom they are associated. It feels safer to dress up in mother's clothes than to be close to mother. More subtly, these conditions for the expression of eroticism may be confined to a secret fantasy elaboration rather than being acted out in reality, with the fantasy being necessary to sexual functioning and orgastic capacity.

When struggles for power are central to the relationship with the emotionally salient parent, power will often become eroticized, and domination and submission will be the vehicle for sexuality rather than love and tender passion.

The perception of parental power changes over time. Initially it is vested in the primary caretaker and symbiotic partner who is usually the mother. This begins with the helpless and powerless infant's participation in the omnipotence of its mother. Gradually the child emerges from the symbiotic orbit, experiencing his or her separateness to an increasing degree. With the realization of the relative powerlessness of the self with relationship to the parent, who is now perceived as the container of all the power, issues of power may become exaggerated in the unsatisfactory relationship, thereby becoming eroticized at the point of genital ascendancy.

In the effort to individuate further from the mother, the child will most often turn toward the father who then is perceived as the container of greatest power. Certainly this pattern has long been supported by traditional sex roles and attitudes, but we can see this propensity apart from social factors both inside and outside the family. Power is intrinsic to the parental role by virtue of the disparity of age alone, and how and where it is perceived is affected by a variety of factors, some social and some developmental. The father, who at the point of the child's genital ascendency is perceived as powerful, is also often idealized and romanticized. Many people assume that women are drawn to men who in some way, obvious or subtle, resemble their fathers. This may be true at one level. Yet at another, as Freud (1931) noted, while a woman's husband is meant to be the inheritor of her relationship with her father, in reality he becomes the inheritor of her relationship with her mother. This is particularly so when the little girl's relationship with her mother was more salient due to a heightened degree of anxiety in that relationship, even though her relationship with her father was less conflicted and more satisfying. If the child's emotional attention is riveted on her mother, the quality of that relationship may come to provide the emotional climate and format for the interpersonal expression of her adult sexuality. On the other hand, if her emotional attention is riveted on her father, the quality of that relationship will tend to be what is replicated.

Power and pride, powerlessness and shame, figure prominently in situations in which parents did not use their real, formal, and attributed power in a benevolent fashion. The need to achieve power and to overcome powerlessness and humiliation becomes a driving force, and, in certain cases, will become eroticized.

The concept of identification with the aggressor is understood in terms of choosing to be the one who *does* rather than the one who is *done unto*—to be the aggressor rather than the victim. The reversal allows for the experience of power, albeit an illusory power based on that very identification with the powerful persecutor.

A homosexual man who recalled bitterly the pain and humiliation of being administered enemas by his father, who would pin him down on the bathroom floor to do it, was intensely excited at the fantasy or act of anal penetration of his sexual partner. Under no conditions would he play the role of the submissive participant.

In fact, being given enemas figures prominently in the erotic fantasies of many people who were subjected to this procedure repeatedly over the early years by mothers who were fanatics about "cleaning out the insides"—mothers who, in great probability, were acting out erotic fantasies of their own in this interaction. For some children it is tantamount to repeated anal rape by a powerful, phallic mother. As such, it is a veiled form of sexual abuse. These fantasies are sometimes played out in adult relationships. If one peruses certain newspapers that carry advertisements for partners to share in a variety of sexual activities, one will come across this interest. Some men, who were victims of this form of maternal power, enjoy turning the tables and forcing anal intercourse upon their wives. They are now the powerful penetrators.

The child who must develop strategies to control an unavailable or inconsistent mother may learn the tactic of sexual seduction that has as its underlying energy source, the excitement of conquest of the unavailable other. The undoing of the anxiety and shame of powerlessness is, in itself, intoxicating. Budding eroticism becomes interwoven in the child with this way of being with the powerful parent; then, in adulthood, seduction becomes the vehicle for conquest of unavailable others, and, symbolically, of the mother. The Don Juan and his female equivalent play out this pattern compulsively in order to undo the sense of powerlessness in their relationships, and the accompanying feelings of anxiety and shame. The unavailability of the powerful parent brings anxiety where there is not a sense of intrinsic power to sustain the individual's sense of security from within.

For every Don Juan there is a perfect partner, the woman who is turned on by the intensity of his pursuit. As one woman put it, "It's what excites me. I'm the focus of intense energy." Although she adored her father, she was anxiously focused on not upsetting her volatile and punitive mother. The experience of being so intensely desired by a man who needed to capture her as ardently as she needed to be captured, undid the anxiety and shame of the powerlessness of her situation with regard to her mother—that is, her inability to command the mother's loving attention and interest.

In the many situations in which a little girl moves normally toward her father in the developmental struggle to disengage from the earlier dependency on her mother, the relationship with him becomes more salient. What is characteristic of the relationship with him is what becomes eroticized. This might, for example, take the form of intensely shared intellectual interests. As an adult she may thus find herself turned on by a man's mind, especially if it is perceived as more powerful than her own.

With the rejection of the mother, who was previously experienced as the powerful other, the father inherits the mantle, and the eroticizing of paternal power will be a common outcome. Women who hold onto this idealized and sexualized perception of male power may not develop their own intrinsic power, choosing instead to be the perennial "power behind the throne." Not until and unless they give up the desire to be special to the father figure—and give up the need to gain their sense of power and pride only through that specialness—and then negotiate the adolescent developmental task of the "overthrow" of parental authority, with all the attendant emotional conflicts, will they be able to integrate their own intrinsic power and relate to men on a more equal basis. But even if the woman works these developmental issues through and is no longer conflicted about them it is very likely that, in the arena of sexual love, the perception of her partner as sexually powerful will be a prerequisite of her erotic response.

When the mother actively refutes her daughter's admiration of her father by criticizing and undercutting him, the little girl may develop contempt for his seeming powerlessness, and may be unable to find her sense of pride and power through being special to him. Although she loves him, his powerlessness may endanger her own sense of power and her self-esteem. She will be pulled back toward the perceived power of the mother. It will be the quality of that relationship with the critical, narcissistic mother, rather than with the more loving father, that will be sexualized and played out in adult sexual relationships. She may be drawn to critical and undercutting men to whom she attributes the power she perceived in her mother, rather than to men who are more loving as was her father. Sometimes love is not enough; certainly not when it is experienced as antithetical to one's power and pride.

From the point of view of what is adaptive rather than maladaptive, the issue is not whether power has become eroticized. Instead, it is whether power issues have to be played out, possibly destructively, in reality, or whether they can exist instead at the level of fantasy and play. Playing at being spanked is a far cry from being truly beaten or humiliated, in which case fear and rage will inevitably contaminate the relationship. The playful act may provide the sense of power that comes with the mastery of what was once a traumatic experience. In addition, the degree to which the acting out becomes compulsive or obsessive marks the difference between the acting out of eroticized power conflicts and the resolving of them in a manner that allows for their expression in modified and symbolic form, free of the hate and fear of the early traumatic interactions.

13

*Power Dynamics
of the Couple*

Almost all children, male and female, share a common history, a common experience that sets the stage for later conflict between men and women. They are all born to and (usually) raised by women. All experience the epitome of helplessness and dependency on a female figure in their early formative years. It does not matter whether she is the best of mothers—the reality for the child is the same. Whatever power and potential threat may come from father later on, it is mother who has the power to give or withhold that which the child, utterly dependent, needs or desires. She has the power to say yes or no, and beyond protest, there is little the child can do to change that reality. It is mother's angry voice and scowling face that terrifies and has become known throughout world literature as the voice and face of the bad witch who has the power to devour and destroy the helpless child. It is the mother who is the object of the little boy's first sexual yearnings and who, no matter how sensitively and understandingly, inevitably must frustrate and shame him. The adversary stance is mitigated for the little girl, for she can identify with her mother and through this identification can assume some of her symbolic power. If we watch a group of small girls playing house, we see how this is practiced over and over in the recreated family drama. The little boy cannot pretend to be the powerful mother without serious repercussions. To identify with the mother is to abandon his maleness. He must identify with the father and then perhaps take on the power conferred on the

110

father in the family structure and upon men in general in the culture. But underneath there is an unconscious (or conscious) fear of the universal mother, the female of all ages. This primordial fear of women has played its role throughout history, motivating physical and political dominance by the male, and sometimes his attempt at psychological dominance as well. To control the eternal mother is to make sure one is never abandoned and never humiliated—two fundamental terrors of the psyche of all men and women, but particularly experienced in the male-female relationship.

In a perhaps unattainable Utopia, both partners of the couple will be secure in their own intrinsic power and will not have to strive for defensive or compensatory power within the relationship. There will be no need to achieve power over the partner to make up for a previous position of powerlessness vis-à-vis one's parents in a symbolic turning of the tables. The decision-making process will entail negotiation instead of a pattern of domination and submission. Neither partner will have to aggrandize the self at the expense of the other.

But the ideal is difficult to achieve in reality. Power issues are likely either to pop up here and there or to flourish in abundance in the interpersonal microcosm of the dyad, whether inside or outside of marriage. Since the marital relationship is in large part a self-contained system—although it does interact with the larger system of the family as a whole—it becomes a hothouse for the flowering of power politics. These rather quickly take root in the character of the relationship, and in the manner in which the partners relate.

The subtleties of the power struggle most frequently are channeled into one or both of the two arenas where these battles appear to take place—sex and money. These may be the most dramatic and highly charged emotionally, so they may act as lightning rods for the discharge of the more subtle underlying power dynamics. Sex can be forced, as in marital rape, or it can be withheld with tactics of impotence by the man or the classic headache of the woman. The doling out or withholding of money by the controller of the pursestrings is a common power strategy, as is the retaliatory profligate spending of the other. Abuse of charge accounts can be a polite way to make an obscene gesture.

The seat of power may not be evident to the naked eye. It may be something that is felt or attributed rather than something that is actually done *to* the other. However, behaviors that are damaging to the relationship may result in an attempt to rid oneself of the shame or anxiety that accompanies the *feelings* of powerlessness.

Therefore, the casual observer may be fooled by blatant behaviors that belie the actual situation. For example, Harry rules with an iron hand. His wife and children appear to be submissive and compliant. Yet, the more careful observer will note the message she sends to the kids with her her eyes—"We'd better humor the jerk." Theirs is a secret collusion of psychological power that, in effect, annihilates his brute control. If we look closer, we may even discover that Harry feels this intuitively. Humiliated and enraged at being mocked, excluded, and made impotent, he may redouble his efforts to control in the only way he knows how.

Larry, who sees himself as a generous and thoughtful husband, cannot understand why his wife is chronically dissatisfied when, as he points out, he lets her have and do whatever she wants. "You LET me?" Marilyn screams. "What do you mean, you LET me?" Larry just doesn't get it. How can a woman who gets everything she wants be so angry?

Marilyn protests the power over her that is implicit in his stance of giving permission. It is the issue of power per se that infuriates her, not what Larry does with it. But Larry's parental stance toward her, albeit that of a *generous parent,* dovetails with Marilyn's readiness to *attribute* parental power to her husband. She regains a sense of power in the bedroom, the area of distress that brought them to counselling in the first place

The definition of the relationship—who has the power and under what circumstances—is set pretty much from the start. However, what is romanticized at the stage of falling in love is often complained about later on. Marilyn found Larry's protectiveness to be reassuring at first. It made her feel safe and taken care of. She also found the aura of the powerful man to be sexually exciting. But the same protectiveness and readiness to take charge evolved into what Marilyn later relabelled *domination,* to which she then felt forced to submit.

Rosalie, on the other hand, was drawn to Leonard's unspoken emotional needs, and from the start she lent herself to making him happy. She was unaware of her own motive to earn his love and concern by taking care of him. She also felt herself to be in the more powerful position of the one who gives rather than the one who needs. Over time she became increasingly dissatisfied with the one-sided nature of their relationship, inasmuch as Leonard was characteristically bound up with his own needs and unconcerned with those of others. Rosalie began to feel powerless, experiencing his ungivingness as a willful withholding. Nothing had actually changed in the outward way in which they interacted. What had changed was how she experienced the locus of power. It was not the felt emotional deprivation that generated her anger. It was the sense of being controlled by a malevolent power, which stirred up old feelings she had in regard to her cold and unsympathetic mother.

Harriet and her husband Roger have another kind of power conflict. Harriet describes how she gets him to stop his critical verbal assaults. She says she makes herself into nothing. She apologizes and asks for forgiveness and criticizes herself even more severely than he has already done. "I let him think he has power over me. That seems to be what he needs." She realizes that there is power in her victim stance, that it stops him from doing what he is doing. And, she acknowledges, it also preserves her secret self who feels very powerful: "I'm afraid to be yelled at, and this is the only way to get any power."

While Harriet's overt powerlessness seems to support Roger's need to be the powerful one, her covert power actually negates his. Her apparent collapse under his attack makes him feel guilty, and he tries to atone by giving in to her demands.

This outward shift in the balance of power leads to feelings of submission and humiliation on his part, to which he subsequently reacts with attempts to regain the upper hand by his critical undermining of her self-esteem. And so on . . . and so on. . . .

The threads of power manifest in outward behavior and hidden in the secret recesses of the mind become twisted and knotted, damaging the fabric of a relationship, sometimes beyond repair.

A sense of safety and self-esteem within the couple relationship is intimately connected with power—who has it and under what conditions, and how it is used. Is it experienced as benevolent or malevolent? Is it willingly shared or is it one-sided? Must it be wrested from the other by force or manipulation, or stolen by secret strategies?

The prevalence of power dynamics will color and shape all aspects of relating within the couple relationship. Until what appear to be substantive issues can be divested of the overlay of power implications, they cannot be successfully resolved.

14

The Need for Power and Symptom Formation: Addiction, Suicide, and Eating Disorders

Striving for power is usually motivated by a need to defend against perceived dangers or to overcome perceived deficiencies. Perceived dangers evoke anxiety, whereas perceived deficiencies stir up shame. To be sure, one may seek power in the service of higher aims, such as the achievement of political power in order to achieve certain social goals, or professional power in order to be able to help others. Hopefully, in these situations, the striving for power has been more or less cleansed of a more private need—to be powerful, and to win, at all costs. This transcendence of personal need is referred to as *sublimation*. Sublimation is the process in which the original defensive reasons for the need for power operate less and less and are finally taken over by higher goals and values. When there is a failure of sublimation, the original need to win, to control, to dominate, is likely to take precedence over social goals and values as a determinant of behavior. The public welfare is likely to suffer when private needs mar judgment and shape decisions. When this happens one will not be able to negotiate or compromise when compromise is necessary. Nor will one be able to cooperate when such behaviors evoke feelings of helplessness or inadequacy and their associated rage or shame in the individuals who must participate in these processes.

In some situations, defensive and compensatory power-seeking leads to the formation of behaviors that are labelled *symp-*

116

toms. These symptoms may take the form of addictive or self-destructive behaviors.

Gambling and Drugs

A child who experiences the mother's power negatively, or whose mother was inconsistent in her availability, may develop a need to control her power that becomes manifest symbolically. For the compulsive gambler, Lady Luck is the elusive mother who is to be magically brought under control, to be forced to give the *supplies* (winnings) which the child had so desperately needed.

The use and abuse of drugs can sometimes have a similar dynamic. The mother who fails to comfort can be brought under control symbolically in the form of a substance that can be ingested whenever the person so chooses. Ironically, those who become addicted, instead of being able to *control the powerful "mother,"* are now controlled by the powerful drug.

Suicide

Suicide is the ultimate last word. It renders everyone else powerless. It is often an act of aggression toward other persons that prevents any possible retaliation. A young man told of his fantasy of fatally shooting himself on the doorstep of his parents' home, so that when they opened the door, they would stumble over his body.

Suicide is also a perversion of will. It says, "I may not be in charge of anything else about life—but this I can control—my own living and my own dying." The would-be suicide not only feels powerless with respect to the outer world, but also within himself. Unlike "The Unsinkable Molly Brown" who says "I ain't down until I say I'm down," the suicide lacks the sense of intrinsic power from which stems not only self-esteem, but hope.

The threats that motivate strategies of power or control may come from within the individual as well as from the external environment.

Threats from Within

Young children sometimes develop in environments in which their own feelings or impulses, or their dependent needs and wishes, lead to their being emotionally overwhelmed. They may become vulnerable to external dangers such as an abusive or critical parent, or one who is intrusive and overrides the child's feelings and will. These children may develop techniques for gaining power over the very feelings, impulses, and wishes that put them in jeopardy. They may deny need and develop a pseudoself-sufficiency. At the same time there is likely to be a chronic underlying depression because of the unmet although unconscious dependency needs and wishes. The inability to experience feelings may interfere with their establishing close and gratifying relationships. Or, in some cases, the cut-off emotions may lead to the development of psychosomatic symptoms, such as high blood pressure or colitis.

In the process of psychotherapeutic treatment of symptoms that arise from a person's need to have power and control over feelings, impulses, and needs, the issue of control will be evident. With an exploration of the dangers that lie behind the need for power over the self, relinquishing this control in the context of a supportive and safe relationship will enable an integration of these various aspects of a whole self.

Power and the Bodily Self

The child's first awareness of a self comes through its physical being. The realization that something is not part of its own body is the first distinction the child makes between self and non-self. Its first attempts to define its own will and intrinsic power will be around bodily functions. Even at the start of life, we see the infant spit out the nipple when it has had enough to eat. It turns its head aside in the primitive forerunner of the universal *no*-gesture, the shaking of the head from side to side. Power struggles around eating and toileting arise in the earliest years when primary caretakers are unwilling to allow a sufficient degree of expression of the child's will and self-determination in these areas alongside the inevitable constraints of the socialization process. The eating disorders are usually a manifestation of disturbance in the fundamental balance of power between mother and child from the start, often culminating in adolescence with the development of symptomatic behavior.

Sours (1980) describes *anorexia nervosa* as a flight from the controlling mother and calls the anorectic's determination "a caricature of will." He writes, "The anorectic struggles against feeling enslaved, manipulated, and exploited. She believes that she has not been given a life of her own. . . . Her goal is power, expressed by a grand gesture which gets its energy from the fact that it is difficult to stop anyone from starving herself." A young woman told me, "I'd reject food to get power and to make her [the mother] fix it the way I wanted it."

The power of the anorectic is delusional insofar as it is dependent on a gross denial of reality that may lead to death. It is a power that comes from opposition, from the no-saying that is particularly characteristic of the second year of life. She[1] not only says no to her mother; she says no to the biological demands of her own body that are now felt to be as alien to her self as were the demands of her mother. She focuses on being her idea of perfect and omnipotent so that she will need nothing and no one outside of her own self.

---

[1]Anorexia has been observed more commonly in females although it is also seen in males. A prolonged emotional and psychological symbiosis is more likely to be resisted by the young boy because of its threat to his gender identity.

The "No, I won't eat" or the "No, I won't go to the bathroom" may constitute the child's first statements of defiance of parental power. He or she may not be able to control the parent, but may believe he or she can at least control what comes into or goes out of his or her own body. When parents cannot tolerate these statements of self-determination, and override them by force, the child is rendered totally powerless and is humiliated by this very impotence. Later in life, individuals who have had this experience in the early years will be likely to resist with all the power they have at hand what they feel to be the demands and intrusions made on them by others. What they experience as attempts to control them will elicit rage, and active or passive resistance.

Eating Disorders and the Need–Fear Dilemma

The eating disorders are disorders of human relationships which have been displaced to the arena of food, of appetite and hunger—submission to it or defiance of it.

The need–fear dilemma refers to the child's conflict between an intensely felt need for the primary caretaker, who is usually the mother—as well as anyone who may later take the place of the mother emotionally—and intense fear of closeness with that person. The first substitute for the mother is the father, and the need–fear dilemma can arise in that relationship as well, especially when the mother is not emotionally available as a safe haven.

The fears that are generally associated with closeness to the primary attachment mother, the one from whom the child must differentiate to become a fully separate and autonomous self, are fears associated with the dangers of engulfment—of being annihilated by the mother's very presence, by the intensity of her needs and emotions. The boundaries of the self attempting to become whole and integrated are threatened, and this in turn motivates distancing strategies by the child in order to provide some degree of control and power against the dangerous mother. The child may learn to hide its real self behind a false facade. Unfortunately, this defense does not do away with the emotional needs for support, nurturance, safety, and self-esteem that are generally supplied by the parent. These intense needs go underground, but continue to press to be heard and expressed in one form or another. Also buried with these needs is the rage that goes with not being responded to, and at the child's being violated or swallowed up by the mother. The child becomes fearful of these needs, not only because they render her vulnerable to the dangers of closeness with her mother, but because they are accompanied by the rage that causes deep anxiety lest it be acted out destructively toward the mother who is also so deeply needed. To be powerful and not have any needs at all becomes the highest priority. The anorectic who fights to maintain a basic sense of her own will must deny the hungers of the body, since to give in to them will confront her with the limits of her power.

As with anorexia, bulimia is a disorder of human relationships which has been displaced to the arena of eating. However, the bulimic is not as successful at denying needs that assert themselves regularly as is the anorectic. The intensity of the need–fear dilemma is consciously felt from two sides, as the bulimic is more commonly troubled not only by her relationship with her mother, but that with her father as well. Needs conflict with fear in both of these basic interpersonal situations.

What is most commonly found in the case of bulimia is that the father's erotic involvement with the daughter, whether as actual incest or in the form of seductive behavior, including eroticized stroking, appeared to be the major danger associated with closeness to him. The father is also overly interested in the daughter's physical appearance, being as obsessively concerned with her gaining weight as she is. Often "gaining weight" refers in fact to the gaining of hips and breasts, the mark of her adult female sexuality which is a provocation for further incestuous feelings on the part of both daughter and father. Although these feelings are not unusual in normal development, in the healthy father-daughter relationship they are not overtly acted out by the father either implicitly or explicitly. The incest barrier is respected, and affectional closeness is not eroticized. The father can be counted on as safe even if the daughter has sexual feelings for him. She knows they will not be exploited.

If the daughter who is frightened by the incestuous dangers with her father cannot rely on her mother to protect her, or to be available for her emotionally so she will not feel forced to go to him for affection or support, she is between the proverbial rock and hard place. To turn to her mother is to experience emotional abandonment and rage. To turn to her father is to experience sexual dangers. She may try to deny needing either one of her parents, but may not be successful in this attempt to keep herself safe. She is more likely to hide her true self and to behave in an adaptive and compliant manner with those who are the recipients of her dependency strivings. In this case she will relate with a pseudocloseness that hides her actual emotional detachment, her barrier *against* closeness. Though she may feel herself pulled toward the other, her real self will not let the other in. She takes in and gets rid of at the same time, acts out the wish and retroactively denies it by "un-doing" it. She stuffs herself with food and forces herself to vomit it out. Inasmuch as emotional *taking in* has both nurturance and sexual implications, eating becomes doubly conflicted.

An obsession is a particular defense mechanism that allows the individual to focus all the anxiety of an interpersonal conflict on a substitute, on a symbolic behavior that distracts the individual from what he or she cannot bear to be aware of directly. The eating disorders are obsessions; they afford the individual a sense of control and power over feelings, needs, and fears, and over the other who is represented symbolically by food.

The obsession with perfection of the body that is characteristic of those with eating disorders is a manifestation of an illusional, grandiose, and powerful self that has to be this way so that the individual will not have to rely on anyone else. If the self is not perfect and omnipotent, how can it be relied on? Failure of this illusion confronts the individual with the fact that she cannot rely totally on herself, and thus the need for the other becomes awakened, exposing her to the interpersonal dangers once again. The striving for power over the self and its physical and emotional needs, for power over the imperfections and frailties of the self, whether physical or moral, and for power over the other who can abandon, swallow up, or sexually exploit the self, often leads to the symptom of an eating disorder. The need–fear dilemma and the defenses against it must be resolved if the individual is to be able not only to give up the food obsession, but also to give up the flight from human relationship which the symptom also represents.

15

Power and the World of Fantasy

Some children who feel themselves caught in the web of a family system that keeps them in a position of powerlessness and shame, take recourse to a secret fantasy life. Here, they may be a benevolent Superman or Wonderwoman who saves the world and earns everyone's love and admiration. Others, more suffused with rage at this situation, become an all-powerful tyrant who rules with an iron fist and tortures and beheads all who oppose him. The regaining of the safety and exalted pride of omnipotence is all that matters, rather than the achieving of the love of others.

These fantasies of being the keeper of either benevolent or malevolent power usually become more sophisticated and elaborate over time, but the basic thrust of the scenario is the same. The individual may settle for a marginal and disappointing life because all needs are satisfied in the secret world of the imagination. Compensatory power becomes so gratifying that the individual does not make the necessary efforts to achieve healthy goals and ambitions in reality.

Describing the "fictive personality," Martin (1988) writes of Don Quixote:

> He lost or suspended his own unsatisfactory self and replaced it with the character, thoughts, feelings, and actions created by others. Something splendid, as well as something frightening, happened to him as a result. [p.12]

The creation of a "fictive personality" may function as both a defense against and compensation for feelings of powerlessness. Martin cites a poem written by John Hinckley, Jr., the young man who attempted to assassinate President Reagan (p. 51). One verse reads:

> *This gun gives me pornographic power.*
> *If I wish, the president will fall!*
> *And the world will look at me in disbelief,*
> *All because I own an inexpensive gun.*

Hinckley, according to Martin, was the youngest of three children. He could never measure up either to his older siblings or to his father. He was described as "so normal, he appeared to fade into the woodwork."

Hinckley filled his empty life with fantasy and finally came to identify almost totally with the main character of the movie, *Taxi Driver*. Our culture offers ample opportunities and models for those who feel powerless and who, enraged at having to be in that position, seek to turn the tables.

The world of fantasy is often the last secret refuge of the person who feels humiliated and powerless to achieve reality-based power and pride.

Sometimes power fantasies bring together power and hate with themes of raw sadism. The fusion of power and hate may be further condensed with sexuality, allowing fantasies of torture to evoke sexual arousal and orgasm. Sometimes the fantasies reveal along with the wish for power the conflict between love and hate. Frequent themes center around the heroic rescue of loved ones from terrible danger or humiliation. For example, an individual may imagine that his parents have been taken prisoner and are being tortured. He fights his way past the guards single-handedly and unties his parents. They fall into his arms, sobbing gratefully. In this fantasy, the imaginer can feel both powerful and good, denying the authorship of that chapter of the fantasy that put his parents in grave peril and pain in the first place. His fantasies overcome and assuage the guilt of his earlier wish to hurt his parents.

The balance between love and hate fluctuates from one extreme to the other, but in all these fantasies vanquishing of fear, pain, and humiliation of powerlessness is the common denominator. In fantasies where the person is the victim of someone else's cruelty, there is a sense of moral superiority and power that comes, perhaps, in dying nobly and well. One is reminded of Billy Budd's last words to the captain who ordered him to be hanged. "God bless Captain Vere!" And in this last act of sweetness he morally defeats Claggart who had set about to destroy him.[1]

Some fantasies are vengeful scenarios in which old defeats and humiliations are redressed. The person achieves great success and honor, while those who originally humiliated him are now part of the crowd clamoring for his autograph. How many returns to high school reunions are simply motivated to show former classmates who always regarded one as a creep what a successful adult one has become. How pleasant it may be to learn that the erstwhile big man on campus is a dismal failure, not to mention the fact that the beauty queen who spurned one's advances now weighs 250 pounds and wears glasses. The universal need to undo early humiliations spawns movies like *The Revenge of the Nerds*. Browsing at the bookstore, one finds *Sue the B*st*rds: the Victim's Handbook*. It promises to tell the reader "How to Get Revenge, Satisfaction and Your Money Back. . ."[2]

Thurber's classic story of *The Secret Life of Walter Mitty* juxtaposes Mitty's meek submission to his wife's nagging control, with his secret world where all are in awe of his skill, power, or bravery. The story begins:

> "We're going through!" The Commander's voice was like thin ice breaking. He wore his full-dress uniform, with the heavily braided white cap pulled down rakishly over one cold gray

---

[1]Herman Melville, *Billy Budd* (1890).
[2]Douglas Matthews, *Sue the Bastards* (1973).

eye. "We can't make it sir. It's spoiling for a hurricane, if you ask me." "I'm not asking you, Lieutenant Berg," said the Commander. "Throw on the power lights! Rev her up to 8500! We're going through!" The pounding of the cylinders increased: ta-pocketa-pocketa-*pocketa-pocketa-pocketa*. The Commander stared at the ice forming on the pilot window. He walked over and twisted a row of complicated dials. "Switch on No. 8 auxiliary!" he shouted. "Switch on No. 8 auxiliary!" repeated Lieutenant Berg. "Full strength in No. 3 turret!" shouted the Commander. "Full strength in No. 3 turret!" The crew, bending to their various tasks in the huge, hurtling eight-engined Navy hydroplane, looked at each other and grinned. "The Old Man'll get us through," they said to one another. "The Old Man ain't afraid of hell!". . .

Then the voice of reality breaks in.

"Not so fast! You're driving too fast!" said Mrs. Mitty. "What are you driving so fast for?"

Stories about the triumph of good over evil, of the weak over the strong, are stories that endure and inspire. Little David defeats the giant Goliath with his slingshot. Jack cuts down the beanstalk, killing the evil giant who pursues him. Hansel and Gretel manage to outsmart the witch and push her into the oven, the fate *she* had in store for them. And Dorothy, terrified for her friend the Scarecrow and angry at the Wicked Witch of the East who had set him afire, saves the Scarecrow and destroys the witch with the same pail of water.

Whether in fables, literature or theater, the unredeemed defeat of the hero is unbearable. The reader or the theatergoer identifying with the protagonist would not be able to tolerate such total powerlessness and humiliation that would feel like his or her own. The tears that flow freely from most who stand in front of the Viet Nam War Memorial in Washington, D.C. speak to the kind of unbearable anguish that finds surcease in the world of fantasy where the meek do, finally, inherit the earth.

16

Criminality

A less benign example of the need for power is that of the criminal personality. Nowhere does the need for compensatory power show itself more clearly than in the criminal mind. In their research, Yochelson and Samenow (1976) found the basic characteristic of these individuals was an underlying feeling of being a nothing, a zero, whose existence is permanently futile. The antidote for this intolerable state is the exertion of power and control over others. They note that "To ask the criminal to surrender his insatiable quest for power and control is to ask him to deprive himself of oxygen" (Vol. II, p. 284). The authors show how closely tied the sense of one's own existence and identity (the "I Am") is to a sense of intrinsic power. In all relationships, the individual with a criminal personality is concerned only with who controls whom. They write about the criminal youngster's triumph because he does not cry when he is whipped.

In his account of the psychology of murder, Macdonald (1986) recounted his interviews with a convicted killer. He noted that when the young man talked about the murder, he made many references to his power over his victim. Finally he revealed to Macdonald that "I talk bad shit like I'm a tough guy. I ain't, I'm scared of everybody." Macdonald adds that the man continued his threatening behavior in the state penitentiary, and that within a few months was himself killed there.

In other species, when two animals are in a fight to the

death, the obvious loser may "expose the jugular," offering an easy kill to the victor. With the loser's gesture of surrender, the winner can simply walk away, sparing the life of the less-fortunate animal. The idea is not to kill. It is to win: to prove to be the most powerful. Once this is done, the killing is unneccesary.

A woman was walking along a dark street when she was approached and threatened by a young man with a knife. In a depressed and despairing frame of mind, she opened her coat wide and said, "Here. Kill me." The young man looked startled, and after a brief moment he ran away without touching his intended victim. With the reversal of who it was that wanted the killing done, there was also a reversal of power. His need to demonstrate his power had been thwarted, and he was frightened by the emergence of his own feelings of impotence.

Yochelson and Samenow (1976) report that the person with a criminal personality may have secret grandiose fantasies of being the greatest in one endeavor or another. The legitimate power that a lawyer or doctor or businessman may have is not enough. He always wants more, "and so he violates to get excitement" (Vol. I, p. 237). It is notable here that excitement is linked with the experience of power. The authors cite the excitement of the arsonist who has the power of life and death over others, who takes pleasure in being able to make a lot of people scream. In all his activities and relationships, the objective is to conquer and possess.

In his classic study of murderers, Bjerre (1927, 1981) wrote of their hate: "It was the hate of the weak, suffering, and incompetent for all strong, happy, self-assured persons: it grew out of fear and envy, and in the last resort out of a sense of helplessness and inferiority, a consciousness of unfitness for the struggle of life." He noted that their "sense of powerlessness and inferiority in the presence of all human beings without exception" was the pre-eminent destructive force within them. He described how their sexuality could not be tied to any conception of love, and wrote of one notorious killer that "his pleasure in every new sexual connection was based on the imaginary belief that his mistress of the moment was completely in his power and that she must yield, even to the point of death, to his all-conquering whims" (p. 117).

This same element of the motivating wish for power may be present in the sexuality of more normal appearing individuals, either in the way they relate to their partners or in the secret fantasies they must spin in their minds in order to function adequately or to reach orgasm.

Macdonald (p. 174) reports the statement of a man with necrophiliac fantasies. "He described with relish the feeling of power and security that he could enjoy in making love to a corpse; it is there when wanted, you put it away when finished with it, it makes no demands, it is never frustrating, never unfaithful, never reproachful. . . . In his sexual relations with women he demanded immobility and compliance."

Macdonald also reported a case of homosexual necrophilia. After murdering his friend the killer said, "I do not think anything would have stopped me. I was mad with power. . . ."

Schafer (1954) found in his analysis of the Rorschach records of sadistic personalities, a theme of power and the subjugation of others.

The major difference between relatively harmless power games of everyday life and the malignant striving for power of the criminal personality is probably directly proportional to the degree of fear, humiliation, and rage behind it. The more abuse and shame that power must make up for, the more abusive and humiliating it will be.

17

Defensive and Compensatory Power

Undoing the Past

When children are traumatized by their parents' misuse of power, their powerlessness generates both anxiety and shame. The "undoing" of that powerlessness often becomes a major motivation later in life.

Undoing may either become an attempt to *defend against* powerlessness and its accompanying anxiety and shame, or it may attempt to *compensate for* it. The acting out of these attempts to undo the past leads to relationships that are structured along power lines rather than genuine love or affection.

Compensatory power *makes up for* feelings of shame or humiliation usually associated with being powerless. Defensive power *protects* the person from anxiety-provoking dangers that accompany the lack of power in interpersonal situations. The person leaning on compensatory power may drive a big car; the person using defensive power carries a big stick.

Sometimes a theoretical or philosophical stance may reflect this wish to undo felt powerlessness. Bertrand Russell (1948) wrote that "It never occurred to Nietzsche that the lust for power . . . is itself an outcome of fear."[1]

---

[1]Bertrand Russell, *A History of Western Philosophy* (1948).

A successful businessman told me, "I believe that power corrupts, but I don't act like it does. When people have money or prestige or fame, I see it as proof they are above the norm. That's unrealistic. They aren't above the norm in attributes outside their field. I'm drawn to people with power because of the reflected glory and power. When my self-esteem was low I felt if I could attain power, like money or prestige, I'd feel okay. I derive my okay-ness from power but I'm not really okay."

People are often driven to achieve the symbols of power, which in this culture tend primarily to be money and what money can buy. A twenty-dollar bill deftly slipped into the palm of the *maître d'hôtel* buys instant prestige and a good table. We see public figures for whom enough can never be enough. People like Ivan Boesky, who made millions on Wall Street through insider trading, seem never to be satisfied. Nothing can fill for them the bottomless pit of powerlessness and the associated shame that leads to insatiability. Hundreds of millions of dollars count for nothing. No matter how many shoes Imelda Marcos had, it was never enough.

The same holds for those who seek other kinds of power with drivenness and insatiability. When such figures achieve political and military power, the world suffers. On a smaller but more commonplace scale, when such a person achieves professional or personal power—as within an office or a family system—the members suffer. One young woman referred to her sister as "the beast who ate Pennsylvania."

Compensatory power does not lead to real change within the individual. It is only a cosmetic that covers the blush of humiliation. Serious conflicts in an individual's earliest experiences with the balance of power often result in failure to develop a healthy base of intrinsic power, and a lack of associated good feelings about the self. This may necessitate the development of tactics that will protect the individual from both the anxiety of powerlessness and the shame that goes with it.

Identification with the Aggressor

One of the techniques of undoing is identification with the aggressor. Instead of being the one who is weak, powerless, and afraid, the individual takes on the identity of the powerful other who originally victimized him. Guntrip (1969) notes how the child, in his struggle to develop inner strength, may turn against his actual small, weak self who betrayed him into the power of disturbing adults through his dependency needs. He notes that the child feels weak because he cannot change the external situation to make it better. Sometimes he may identify with the persecutory adults so he can better repress his weak infantile self. He takes on the personality of those who appear as powerful figures in his little world. Guntrip quotes one patient's fantasy of hurting a child. "Wouldn't I love to make it squirm. I'd break every bone in its vile little body, I'd crush it" (pp. 204–205). The cruelty, Guntrip reveals, is cruelty to the despised child within and is the root of all cruel treatment of real children.

From the age of 3 on, John was repeatedly belittled and ridiculed by his father. As a man, John had a Jekyll-and-Hyde character in his relationships with women. In many relationships he was helpful to the point of obsequiousness, and he could also be seductive with his little-boy charm—two ways of "managing" and thus controlling others. But in an intimate relationship, and when he was emotionally significant to a woman, he would become his sadistic father and use his father's techniques of devaluation on her.

He described his mother as "a basket case." It is doubtful that she had been that way when she got married at the age of 20. We tend to forget that an abusive spouse can be as destructive, throughout a marriage, as are abusive parents throughout the formative years. This is especially true in the many cases in which people attribute parental power to their mates. This attributed power may, at the outset, be looked up to and regarded as a potential source of security. This makes the "victim" susceptible to the aggressor. From the point of view of the aggressor, in light of past experiences, the power of the needed other is envied, hated, and feared; and it must, at all costs, be brought down. Furthermore, the very feelings of dependency that are brought into the relationship make the insecure spouse feel very vulnerable and shamed by these feelings, and it becomes imperative to get out of the one-down position.

When individuals come into a long-term relationship with a preexisting degree of insecurity and unsureness about themselves as a result of less-than-favorable early years, they tend to believe the negative messages that may be heaped upon them. A downward spiral of ever decreasing self-esteem is likely to develop. Women are especially vulnerable to attacks upon their physical selves, which may be—as for many men—their basic true self. The partner who criticizes breasts and hips as too big or too small, for example, attacks the symbols of her femininity and her feelings about herself as a woman. This vulnerability is compounded by sociocultural conditioning. With the degree of insecurity that is engendered by this approach, the husband need not keep his wife "barefoot and pregnant." She'll be unable to move out into the world because she has no self-esteem to make such a move possible. She will stay there, under his power, in his control. She will turn into "a basket case."

The aggressiveness may take many other forms, such as an attack upon the intellect, for example. Whatever the vehicle for this tactic, the bottom line is power: how to get it and how to keep it.

Turning passive into active

Playing out the earlier experiences of powerlessness represents an attempt to gain a sense of mastery over them. The child who is harmed by the parental misuse of power may, in symbolic form, do to himself what was once done to him.

In "S and M" sex games, the "victim" knows all along that

this is a game. He can initiate it. He can end it. He can specify how much or how little he is to be hurt. Temporarily, he is in control of the familiar drama. The pleasure is not in being a victim or in feeling pain; the pleasure is in the sense of power that goes with mastery over the situation. It is often assumed that if a person is "masochistic," it is because he enjoys the pain itself. Quite the contrary. He enjoys being sure that the pain will not be more than he can bear.

Sometimes a person who acts out this scenario reports an upsurge of anxiety that the situation might actually get out of his control, and that he might really be hurt. These breakthroughs of anxiety reflect a degree of fear behind the attempt to undo by turning the passive into the active.

The person who identifies with the aggressor does to others what was done to him, gaining an illusion of power by momentarily becoming the powerful figure. The person who turns from passive to active does to himself, or brings about, what was done to him by the powerful figure in his life, thereby gaining an illusion of control.

We-Power

The individual who identifies with the aggressor finds a defensive illusory power by mentally fusing with the *hated* but powerful parent figure; however, another person may find a compensatory illusory power by mentally fusing with an *admired* and powerful other. In both cases, the wish to feel powerful is the major determinant.

Whether we are talking about the zealous followers of an Adolf Hitler, or the frenzied groupies who attach themselves to a rock music star, the phenomenon is one of borrowed power. In this situation, both power and perfection are first attributed to the idol. This is different from the admiration felt by an ordinary fan or political supporter. For despite the strength of their admiration, *these* people are well rooted in their own identity and have other sources of self-esteem. They do not have to seek a compensatory illusory power by joining in an all-encompassing *we*-ness with an idealized figure. In this we-ness, the idol's attributes of power and perfection are experienced as one's own. This idol may be an over-idealized member of one's own family.

A 7-year-old boy who overly identified with his idealized mother commented, when she finished her doctoral dissertation, "We're going to publish it." Surely this was not his idea, but he fused with his mother in her fantasies of fame and success.

Sometimes a person who marries someone successful or well known plays out the same fantasies. The power and perfection attributed to the mate become one's own. This situation can be as mundane as the woman who bases a sense of power and superiority on her identity as a doctor's wife. These people may suffer a traumatic loss of identity and self-esteem if their mates leave them or die. Fusion with one who is perceived as powerful and admirable repairs the felt deficiency in the self, although this repair is dependent upon the external connection. Inwardly there is no real change.

What motivates such an identification is not so much the nature of the emotional link with the other person—love or hate—as the dimension of power and the wish to be powerful that are involved.

18

*Power in the
Psychotherapy
Relationship*

The need to maintain control and the need to create feelings of power in interpersonal relationships become the person's self-protective, defensive reactions to underlying anxieties and insecurities. These anxieties are very often the result of the early caretakers' failure to provide security and self-esteem for the child through the benevolent use of their power. When the power of the other is perceived as malevolent or unreliable in some way, it must be controlled.

This defensive posture in the world, the attempt to manage the interpersonal situation, takes many forms such as seduction, coercion, bribery, intimidation, guilt-inducement, or compliance. Although these techniques may appear to work on one level for a period of time, the other person will inevitably react to being controlled, whether the control is blatant or subtle. In intimate relationships, the locus of power and its expression may become more important than earlier yearnings for love or nurturance. In the world of work, power struggles with superiors may lead to failure to achieve vocational or professional goals. When an individual who is in a position of formal power has this power motive, designated tasks and shared goals may be sacrificed to these personal power needs. Talented subordinates may be rendered impotent; the best employees then leave and there is an overall decrease in the quality of the organization.

In the psychotherapy situation, this defensive posture vis-à-vis others is played out with the therapist. This stance is referred to as "transference resistance" in psychoanalytic terms. It is a way of managing the therapeutic relationship so as to bring about a wished-for interaction and/or to prevent a feared one. By maintaining power over the therapist through these management-techniques, the patient feels safe from the attributed power of the therapist now assumed to be as dangerous as the power of early caretakers and authority figures.

It is the responsibility of the therapist to recognize this behavior and not to enter into inadvertant collusion with the patient. He or she must not be seducible, coercible, or intimidatable, but must try to help the individual understand the fears and anxieties behind his or her need to control the other, behind the need to maintain a fragile sense of power and pride. As these anxieties are confronted and unconscious dangers rendered less frightening, this rigid and limiting manner of relating to others can be relinquished and replaced by healthier, more satisfying relationships.

In Dan Wakefield's article "My Six Years On The Couch," which appeared in a recent Sunday magazine section of the *New York Times,* he said:

> Like many in my generation, I had already made the intellectual substitution of Freud for God. I was seeking from Freudian psychoanalysis the long-lasting, earthly kind of salvation I hadn't gotten from baptism and church and Jesus.

He added that he had entered analysis with the commitment of an acolyte taking vows to a rigorous religious order.

From the start it was clear that Mr. Wakefield had a fantasy of an idealized, powerful other who would make everything all right if he only followed the rules and submitted obediently to that power.

This attitude carries within it the seeds of failure of the therapeutic process UNLESS the attitude itself comes under scrutiny.

In clinical terms, this comes under the heading of "analysis of transference" central to psychoanalytic theory.

Analysis and through it, change in the patient's relationship to his own power, and to others' power past and present, is critical for the achievement of psychological health and maturity that is the goal of treatment. Wakefield's first step toward "cure" came when he finally gave up his fantasy. This was accompanied by a surge of anger at the analyst for his failure to live up to Wakefield's idealization. The failure of the treatment itself was not due to an intrinsic flaw in psychoanalysis. It was due to the analyst's failure to deal effectively with his patient's childish and maladaptive relationship to attributed power. Divested of his illusions, Mr. Wakefield was able to complete the work of his treatment elsewhere.

Power manifests itself in many ways in the therapeutic relationship; sometimes it is actual but more often illusory. The patient presents himself or herself at the therapist's office as needing help of some sort, pays a fee, and is bound by the structure of treatment as defined by the therapist in terms of length of sessions and availability of the therapist's time. The patient exposes his or her private fears, feelings, and fantasies. The therapist does not. The relationship is lop-sided by its very nature. This imbalance sets the stage for the emergence of power issues in the relationship.

Recalling the power differential in the parent-child relationship (which has its parallels in the new therapy situation), the actual power of parents ideally provides a sense of safety and security for the child. The child can go on being a child, certain that its parents will take care of whatever needs to be taken care of. Benevolent power supports growth, allows for the healthy expression of the I Am, I Can, and I Will of the child. Identity, mastery, and intentionality, the core elements of intrinsic power, thrive under the aegis of benevolent parental power. And benevolent parental power is gradually set aside as the child moves toward adulthood and takes control of its own life and destiny.

The same can be said of the benevolent power of a therapist

who provides an arena of safety and security within which the patient can struggle with archaic terrors, conflicts, and hatreds, as well as with love, hope, and creativity. And, as the child must break away from parental power, the patient should be able to emerge from the mantle of the therapist's power, challenging it if necessary, gradually establishing the self as an adult in the therapist's adult world. By the end of treatment, the sense of power differential should be gone, or well on its way to being gone. This can only come about if the therapist has a healthy relationship to his or her own power and that of others, and is sensitive and responsive enough to power issues that trouble the patient.

The patient also brings into the therapeutic relationship attributed power which may be perceived in a variety of ways depending on the individual's previous experience with power. Is the therapist's power to be feared and controlled? Or will the feared power be assuaged by a submissive and compliant stance vis-à-vis the therapist? Or, as with Wakefield, is there a passive submission to power that assumes a reward for such submission? If he is a good boy and goes to church every Sunday, will God love him and take special care of him?

One person said:

I hate being needy. It's a set-up for pain. It makes me furious to need your empathy—the humiliation and powerlessness. I want to be able to rescue *you,* to find something missing in your life. It's hard to have you just be there for me. I have to find something in you so I can seduce you into needing me. That way I will be able to feel in control.

For this person, even benevolent power was dangerous. The very emergence and articulation of these feelings paved the way for his being able to lean on the therapist and feel safe enough to delve into his long-buried agonies.

Some people need to make the good-other bad, because that very goodness makes the person want him or her too much. The desired one has the power to say yes or no, to give or withhold. A way to regain a sense of power and control is to spoil the good other, by finding, for instance, something to criticize. This eradicates both the need for and the felt danger of being in the power of the wished-for good-other. This differs from spoiling that is motivated by envy. I have already reported the dilemma of the patient who felt he had to destroy my "power" because his envy was unbearable.

In another situation, the therapist had begun to address the patient's attitudes towards the power of the therapist which were manifested in complaints. The therapist observed that the patient seemed frustrated with God, as well, because He wasn't helping her. The patient replied:

> God could help, but I'm not important enough. God is so full of Himself that He shows his power by not helping. My father was all puffed up like that.

The therapist wondered if the patient felt that she (the therapist) was also withholding help just to show *her* power. The patient answered:

> There is a power differential here. I need you more than you need me. That became obvious when you went on vacation. But you don't seem to *need* to show your power over me.

If the therapist is to be effective in the area of the patient's power conflicts, he or she has to be comfortable having power without the *need* either to have it or to reject it. If he or she is too uncomfortable with either the actual or attributed power of the situation and needs to equalize the relationship, either by inappropriate self-disclosure or behavior that communicates an absence of power, the patient is then deprived of a useful experience with a benevolent power on whom one can rely and at the same time let down one's own defenses against possible feared psychic pain or dangers. On the other hand, if the therapist's underlying feelings of powerlessness and shame lead him or her to exploit the therapeutic relationship, no matter how beguiling this might be to the patient, then in subtle ways there will be a barrier to the patient's achieving his or her own secure sense of intrinsic power just as there was in childhood and adolescence. The therapist who takes on the mantle of a guru, who thrives on the adoration of many patients may seem superficially benign, but the importance of this position will be obvious to the patient who will then play along by staying small and dependent in order to obtain the love of the idealized parent figure. It is a therapy that can never really end, because the patient is never permitted to grow up, in order that the therapist may continue to maintain his or her own sense of power and pride.

Defeating the Helper

The relationship between a psychoanalyst or psychotherapist and the person who is seeking help is referred to as an "alliance." There are two aspects to this arrangement. One is the "therapeutic alliance" which refers to the atmosphere of basic trust and safety. The second aspect is the "working alliance" which refers to the partnership between therapist and patient in which they undertake the task of therapy, agreeing to be not only participants in the treatment process, but observers of it as well. Sometimes there may be a therapeutic alliance, but a failure to develop a working alliance. However, there cannot be a working alliance without a therapeutic alliance.

Power needs interfere with both aspects of the therapeutic relationship. If these power issues are not directly addressed and understood in the context of the person's character defenses and developmental history, it is likely that they will continue to be played out, consciously or unconsciously, in a way that ultimately will defeat the underlying purpose of the therapeutic endeavor.

Jerry's mother was alternately seductive and rejecting. As a child he suffered from his mother's inconsistent attitude toward him because she neglected his genuine developmental needs. The situation generated such anxiety, frustration, and rage in him that he developed self-protective strategies to control not only authority figures in his growing-up and adult years, but also those women with whom he became emotionally involved. Since his relationships repeatedly failed, he decided to seek the help of a therapist. From the very start, issues of power and control, shame and humiliation, permeated the therapeutic relationship. Putting himself in what seemed like a powerless and humiliating situation because he had to turn to someone else for help, he had to find ways to turn things around, to find subtle ways to embarass or frustrate the therapist or to control the process with his clever intellect. His training as a lawyer made it possible for him to use words and reason to his own power advantage. But sometimes when he let his guard down, the underlying pain would show. Jerry didn't feel better if the therapist showed any concern or empathy. Instead he felt humiliated, exposed, and in a one-down position. Reacting, he would say something sarcastic that would generate feelings of powerlessness and embarassment in the therapist. Jerry thus re-established his dominance of the session and then his sense of both security and pride . . . but he *could not* absorb his therapist's empathic concern and caring. The pained child within was left as frightened and alone as before.

Only when the therapist began to confront the power-maintaining behavior, viewing it as a defense against further feelings of emotional abandonment and shame, could they begin the difficult task of real change. The relationship between them became the focus of their exploration. As Jerry began to stop playing out his defensive power tactics with regard to the therapist, that relationship became a secure and stable one within which Jerry could begin to grow, and change, and develop healthier and more satisfying ways of relating to others.

Consenting Adults

Nowhere does attributed power play a greater role than in the helping professions. The individual who consults a professional helper whether it is a minister, a psychoanalyst, a physician, or even a dentist often does so with a sense that "the doctor" has special powers above and beyond knowledge of a technical nature. "I'm in your hands," is often implied by the individual when consulting such a professional.

Nobody wants to make the dental hygienist angry when she holds a sharp instrument poised at one's gum line. A person may be afraid that the sadistic use of power might pop up in unexpected places. How much is fear of going to the dentist a manifestation of an unconscious distrust of the powerful other? Perhaps it is not the procedures that are threatening as much as the person who wields the instruments. Scenes from *Marathon Man,* with Laurence Olivier hovering menacingly over an unanesthetized Dustin Hoffman, may come to mind at such moments. Furthermore, the more we fear our own latent sadism, which is the use of power to hurt, the more we are likely to fear it in others.

But we cannot go through life in a state of paranoid vigilance, and so we hand over our trust to the people to whom we turn for certain kinds of help. This can include occupations outside of the professions as well. One woman in the survey I reported on earlier put the automobile mechanic in this category, expressing her feelings about how the power of expertise is sometimes used to take advantage of the customer.

One of the most disturbing misuses of the power sometimes attributed to the helping professional is that of sexual exploitation. In regard to a situation in which a sexual encounter has taken place between a psychotherapist and a patient, for example, the therapist may claim, "But she was a consenting adult!" No indeed, it wasn't rape. In fact, there was no protest at all. But was she really a consenting adult? Is the 11-year-old daughter who goes along with her father's sexual wishes because she loves and trusts him a consenting adult? Of course not. Nor is the patient who, although a sentient adult woman, brings the little girl's wishes, fears, and trust to the idealized therapist. In the betrayal of this little girl's trust, the therapist is using his power malevolently; moreover, because of the unconscious implication of incest, sexual relations with a therapist or gynecologist or minister is in the long run, if not immediately, psychologically devastating to the woman. This would be just as true if the patient were a man. The misuse of power in such a situation is as malevolent as the misuse of power by the perpetrator of incest.

The therapy relationship is a microcosm, a special laboratory in which the patient can experience, confront, overcome, transform, or transcend the barriers to satisfying love and work. These barriers often relate to power issues, and the therapy situation offers an opportunity to *confront* these rather than to continuosly act them out in inevitably self-defeating behaviors.

Part IV

Power in
Everyday Life

19

Power in the Workplace

Clearly one setting in which principles of power are operative is the workplace. Here many individuals come together to become an organization. All of them are to be oriented toward achieving the goals and purposes of that organization. It is a situation where there will be leaders and followers, bosses and the people who work under their direction, where individual goals will in large measure necessarily be subverted to those of the organization. This, of course, sets the stage for power attributions that activate parent-child power struggles. One young man described how he deliberately slowed down at his work as a way to gain power. Then he had to deal with his sense of failure at not achieving the level of which he was capable.

Ideally, intrinsic power, based on the skills and talents of the individuals, would far outweigh their needs for compensatory or defensive power. When defensive and compensatory power strivings of one or more individuals become manifest, one can expect that power struggles and personal power needs will interfere with the smooth and effective working of the overall organizational system.

Early Research

In the classic research of Lippitt and White (1958), it was found that the emergence of an individual as a leader depends on how well his particular abilities and traits match a given leadership role. It was found that authoritarian leadership is conducive to apathy or resistance on the part of others, while in a situation of democratic leadership, one finds more originality, less aggression, and more productivity when the leader is absent. One would expect that the higher the level of authoritarianism, the more attributed power will be evoked, with feelings from the power situation in play with the parents now coming to the fore. Parent–child dynamics will be reactivated with respect to power struggles as will be the acting-out of resentment toward the parental figure who interferes with the expression of intrinsic power, and who shames or humiliates those who feel they must submit.

Studies of situations that engendered either cooperation or competition (Deutsch 1960) led to the findings that competition can be decreased by stressing the importance of the group outcome, which can be greater than individual gain and can be achieved by cooperation. Competitiveness increases under situations of threat or when communication is not permitted. Anxiety is likely to call into operation such defenses that allow the individual to feel powerful or in control, setting the stage subsequently for the emergence of long-standing patterns of defensive power-seeking.

Potent Leadership

In *The Tao of Leadership,* Heider (1985) describes "potent leadership." What is significant, he claims, is the ability of the leader to be aware of what is happening in the group and to act accordingly. He believes that specific actions are less important than the clarity of the leader. "Potency cannot be calculated or manipulated, nor is it a matter of trying to look good" (p.75). Heider tells us that leaders who lose touch with what is happening cannot act spontaneously. Instead they try to do what is "right," and if that fails, that may resort to coercion. Coercion sheds no light on what is actually happening and often backfires, generating conflict instead. Heider notes that the wise leader knows better than to be self-centered, or, in the terms of this book, not to add his own personal power needs whether defensive or compensatory. He emphasizes that the well-run group is not a battlefield of egos and that pride or the self-aggrandizement of personal power are not maintained at the expense of the goals and purpose of the organization.

Heider states further that the integrity of the leader is not idealistic. "It rests on pragmatic knowledge of how things work." Like the parent who uses power benevolently, good leadership consists of motivating people to their highest levels by offering them opportunities, not obligations. That is, opportunities reinforce their sense of intrinsic power, of identity, mastery and intentionality, as opposed to obligations that evoke feelings of submission to a dominant and powerful authority. Rather than acting as a punisher, the wise leader knows there are natural consequences for every act, and his/her task is to shed light on these consequences, not to attack the behavior itself. In the workplace, these consequences might be loss of the job if the individual acts in a way that is antithetical to the well-being of the organization or interferes with the pursuit of its goals and purposes. The leader, or manager in this situation, has to be sufficiently comfortable with power to be able to follow through on the prescribed consequences when necessary. He or she cannot be too concerned with being liked or too guilty to be able to act. Organizations where this is the case may find themselves in trouble when there is a gradual accumulation of individuals who do not act on behalf of the organization, where individual power needs or greed affect their work and the plans and strategies that are put into effect. Analogous to Gresham's law that bad money drives out good money are the valuable employees who will leave an organization that becomes weighed down with those whose power issues make it difficult, if not impossible, for them to do their work and to feel the pride and satisfaction in expression of intrinsic power.

Heider points out that the leader must have stability and a

secure sense of self in order to be able to work with erratic people and critical situations. Without these resources, an individual's striving for defensive power begins to operate to protect the sense of safety of the self. "The leader who knows when to listen, when to act, and when to withdraw, can work effectively with nearly everyone," Heider asserts (p.55).

The View from Above

I asked a successful manager who had risen rapidly in an extremely well-functioning and rapidly expanding company for his observations with respect to power in the workplace. His reply (which he had come to intuitively) echoed Heider's wisdoms. His well-developed sense of intrinsic power and the absence of any need for defensive or compensatory power made what Heider calls *potent leadership* come to him naturally. This is what he told me (*my comments appear in italics*):

> There are three levels of power: the line worker, the middle manager, and the executive. How one uses power in the workplace is directly related to one's goals.
>
> If the individual's personality is such that he or she is content to be a line worker without responsibility for others, and there is no wish to move into managerial positions, power comes from doing well on the job. The power of the superior worker rests in the fact that the boss doesn't want to lose him and his ability to say "I quit." This power may bring him certain considerations, as, for example, when the manager bends over backwards to give him the vacation dates he prefers. It is not that he gets more time, but that he gets the time he wants.
>
> The person who wants to climb from the ordinary worker's level to the managerial level is faced with the same basic terms, except that he or she may have to sacrifice those special considerations in the interest of the organization.

There will be a trade-off. He or she must also be ready to quit, in order to advance, if that sacrifice is not recognized. The person has to have the inner security and faith that another and better position will be found elsewhere.

(This security will optimally come from a secure sense of intrinsic power, of I Am, I Can, and I Will rather than from a defensive or compensatory omnipotence or grandiosity.)

The middle manager has to be able to deal with those under him as well as those over him. The power he/she has with people under him is that of control. (*If he is to use this power well and benevolently so that it enhances the overall competitive working towards the goals and purpose of the organization, he will not have a defensive or compensatory* need *to control.*)

The power the middle manager has with people above him in the organization is favor, their good opinion of him (*and his ability to evoke an attitude of benevolent power in them*).

The middle manager must walk a fine line in order to balance the two positions. Power with those over him can be achieved, in part, by the ability to "finesse" delicate situations. For example, the boss sets a goal that the manager knows is counterproductive for the organization. He has made a mistake, and the manager knows it is a mistake, but nevertheless it is a directive. So the manager must begin the task without initial resistance. He shows himself to be a positive supporter of the boss. (*He does not act in a way that may evoke competitive power-striving on the part of the boss.*) He then lets the boss know about each obstacle as it comes up and lets the boss decide if and when to discontinue that course of action. (*In Heider's words, he knows what is happening and sheds clarity on the situation as it happens.*) The middle manager cannot fight his superior and win. He supports him and *then* steers him to a proper conclusion. The one who fights the boss (*and activates a power struggle*) is not likely to climb in the organization. The one who knows how to finesse the situation, to affect the outcome without challenging the power of the boss, is the one who will be in favor.

With those under him, the manager must have the power of control, to be sure the worker is productive, efficient, and happy—that is, not disgruntled and thus likely to act out against the organization. The manager gets this control by 1) listening to what the workers say, and 2) noticing what the workers do. Then the manager lets the workers know *verbally* that he has listened to what they have to say and he lets them know *verbally* that he has noticed what they have done, especially when it is good. (*He functions actively as the benevolent power who enhances the workers' self-esteem, feelings of success, and personal potency—that is, their intrinsic power.*)

When there is an interpersonal problem between workers, the manager must confront the problem *without delay* and must verbalize to all involved, *individually,* the tension that these workers are feeling. He must make them see that the problem is not with the other person but with the tension the other person is making them feel. The manager directs the worker to defeating the tension rather than the other person. (*This recalls what Heider said: that the wise leader does not act as a punisher but knows there are natural consequences for every act, and that it his task to shed light on these consequences and not to attack the behavior itself.*)

For example, two women in the office are close friends. In fact, one got the other one hired. They have a fight outside of the office and as a result are unable to talk or even look at one another. Since they work in the same office, the problem becomes obvious to everyone and attention is diverted to their situation. The tension is felt by everyone and comes to the manager's attention. The manager must talk to each of them individually, stating the problem and what has been observed with respect to the tension. He may ask them if *they* enjoy the tension, and of course they will say they do not. The manager then states the consequences of the tension's erupting into an office fight, pointing out such a fight could lead to the loss of their jobs. However, he then reviews the workers' positive qualities to build self-esteem, and tells them their goal is to overcome that tension before it is too late. The manager may go so far as to suggest specific techniques for tension reduction, such as breathing deeply, thinking of something funny, or, to help them gain a sense of perspective, to think about what is most important in their lives and to compare this issue with it. They are not expected to shake hands when they do not want to although with time this may come to pass. The workplace is equated with the family where people must learn to live together even when individual members may not always like each other. The manager poses acceptance of the other as a work challenge. People who are listened to and who are given challenges will usually meet them. (*When they are neither dominated nor humiliated, they will not have to resort to power techniques to make themselves feel either safe or unashamed.*)

Conflicts of those with power for more power, as when two or more middle managers are vying for the same greater opportunity, will generally be decided on the basis of certain qualities. A major issue is one's willingness to acknowledge the power of the superior and to accept the duties presented with sincerity and diligence. It is all right to state objections as long as it is clear that the duty is also accepted. If there is doubt as to the acceptance of that duty, that is, if the individual does not support the power and authority of the superior, he or she will lose power in the organization. Superiors must trust the individual to do as they say. They will respect objections as long as they know they can count on the person to carry out their directives. One has to be able to suppress the ego—to be able to put aside personal power strivings.

At the executive level, power is generally determined by an additional factor—public opinion—the perception of all those below the executive. With each step up the ladder the number of people below increases geometrically. It is important for the top leader to keep the organization both stable and productive. He or she must campaign daily to be

visible to all below. This may also involve travel. Other demands of the position may be considered a nuisance, but the
person in true power must have public opinion behind him.
When decisions have to be made, chances of opposition will
be slim. For example, a vote put to the shareholders who
stand at the apex of the power triangle, inasmuch as they
have power to fire the chief executive officer if they so decide, will come out in favor of the leader who has the support
and good opinion of those below. The power of the executive lies in the ability to make decisions that affect the largest
number of people and to have their decisions successfully
implemented. The person with most power is the one who
has earned the support and respect of most people.

Failed Power

The picture painted by this manager contrasts with stories from
companies that were failing to achieve their goals, and companies
that were in trouble. In these instances there was, on the part of
some managers, a fear of having power where, because of a wish
to be liked or because of guilt, they were unable to remove individuals who subverted the goals and purpose of the organization.
Talented individuals were blocked by others who, competitively,
needed to keep them in a powerless position lest their own power,
greed, and territory be endangered. These companies were not
thriving and some were in serious trouble. Management at various levels resisted change and were faced with having change
thrust upon them.

Roone Arledge, president of American Broadcasting Company's News and Sports, in a television interview with commenta-
tor Howard Cosell, was asked if he thought that network news
might be *too* powerful. "Does it go so far as to shape the news?"
Arledge replied that power, like the atomic bomb, is only good if
you don't use it. He thought that if the press did use its power to

control the news, it would lose its credibility, and thus, lose the very power it was abusing. This highly successful and powerful man knew that personal power needs are dangerous in any endeavor. Only by keeping them in check and by the cooperative expression of the intrinsic power of many individuals working toward a common goal, can any organization succeed in the pursuit of that goal.

20

Power Tactics

Advocacy

Within the family we sometimes find that a more benign parent has failed to protect the child from the other parent who abuses the power he or she has—perhaps by virtue of being bigger and by claiming the authority of one or another of the parental roles. It is surprising how often, when there has been abuse, more anger is directed at the "good" parent who failed to use his or her power as an advocate for the child. The complexities of the power balance within the marital couple affect the use or abuse of power, or the failure of power vis-à-vis the child. Powerlessness is not much more admirable than power in this context.

An advocate is a supporter or a defender. Advocacy therefore is a manifestation of the benevolent use of power on behalf of others who are relatively powerless. We have a form of government that is designed to provide, through the judicial system, an advocate for the citizen with regard to the other arms of government. It is a sector of government that is designed to protect the people from the misuse of power by the government itself.

We see, in the public domain of the media, various forms of citizen advocacy such as David Horowitz's "Fighting Back," or "Action Line." Built into lower levels of government are agencies, such as the Consumer Protection Agency, whose function is to use its formal power on behalf of those who are powerless against others with higher position or more money.

Power in the form of advocacy reminds us that power per se is neither good nor bad. As much as power may corrupt and as much as it may be abused, it can also be used toward positive and constructive ends.

Silence as a Power Tactic

Many people know only too well what it means to be given "the silent treatment." It is a particularly sadistic form of wielding power.

The seeker is always in a less-powerful position that the one who is sought. The power of "yes, I will," or "no, I won't," may be attempts on the part of the 2-year-old to establish his or her own will and autonomy. On the other hand, the child also knows what it is to be on the opposite side of this particular power balance. The withholding of minimal social interaction as a way to coerce or control or punish, as in the use of silence as a power tactic, strikes at the very heart of the relationship. It says, in effect, "I do not even acknowledge your existence." This is especially devastating, even annihilating, for the young child who is still dependent on his or her parents to define reality.

One woman had been devastated from early childhood on when her mother would not only refuse to speak to her but would also pretend not to see her. The little girl would become frantic, not only because of the totality of the abandonment but because of the threat to her very sense of being, and her utter powerlessness to do anything about it. She would be reduced to begging and pleading which was ignored. She could have no impact. Whatever intrinsic power she might have developed would be wiped out at these times. This same frantic sense of helplessness would come to be experienced in her adult relationships as well.

Teasing

One dictionary definition of the verb "tease" is "to arouse hope, desire, or curiosity without affording satisfaction." It is also defined as "to make fun of; playfully mock."

Teasing is not play and being teased is not fun. The one who is teased is rendered powerless, and in the process is likely to feel shamed or humiliated. The teaser plays out a need for power that carries with it a wish, conscious or unconscious, to do just that— to render powerless and to shame the other person.

Teasing is a form of hostile aggression that is often denied by the teaser with words like, "Hey, it's all in fun. Where's your sense of humor?" The one who is teased is rendered still more impotent when any counteraggression is blocked by the threat of being called a "poor sport."

Teasing is one of many power games. It affords the teaser an illusory and compensatory power that serves to defend against his or her own sense of powerlessness and shame. It is a turning of the tables; now someone else is in the position that the teaser had been in earlier in life. It is as though the powerlessness and shame is taken from the self and put into the other who now has to contain it, and who certainly feels it. This power tactic defends against the anxiety of being powerless, and compensates for the shame of having been in that position.

Criticism

The dictionary defines "criticize" as "to judge the merits and faults of, or to judge with severity." Criticism is the passing of unfavorable judgment, censure, or disapproval.

The very act of criticizing is an act of power. It arrogates to the self the power of the parent. Even praise comes from a superior power position, since it still defines the self as the one who has the power to judge. A genuine appreciation of something that another has done does not come from the judgmental position, and thus is not an act of power. A genuine "Gee! That's great!" feels very different from a pat on the head.

The professional critic of art, drama, or music often has the power to make or break an artistic production or even the artist himself. Sometimes this power is used maliciously and spitefully, and careers are damaged. The critic who is genuinely concerned with artistic merit and not with achieving his or her own compensatory power can help the artist refine the work, although differences in artistic taste have to be taken into consideration.

Criticism in the intimate interpersonal relationship often has more elements of power and control in it than a genuine wish to help the other. Unlike the overt attempts to spoil the other, criticism hides behind a wish to help. As such, the power issues are much more difficult to recognize or to confront.

The criticizer with hidden power motives raises his or her self-esteem by elevating the self to a position superior to the partner—the position of the judge. The act of criticism inevitably defines the other as inadequate or inferior or impotent, and may carry with it an attitude of contempt or disrespect. When this power tactic is used by wives against husbands, as it frequently is, the women are likely to be suffering from painfully low self-esteem developed in the context of their relationships with their mothers. This is not necessarily a man-woman issue, although it is frequently played out in marriage where *all* the parent-child power conflicts become replicated. But whether it is the woman who gains power by being critical of the man, or the man who gains power by being critical of the woman it is true that—as paraphrased earlier in this book—when power comes in the window, love goes out the door.

Within the Ivory Tower

Many people enjoy the fantasy of academic life as lived by a modern-day Mr. Chips, picturing the broad lawns and ivy-covered

Gothic buildings of a small midwestern college, or the greater sprawl of a large university. Academe takes on the image of a peaceful family to whose sheltering bosom one can return, fleeing the harshness of the real world.

Surprise! Power politics respects no walls, ivy-covered or not. The competitive atmosphere, the striving for grant money, appointments, or tenure, for control of a specific department and its policies, create a picture that bears no resemblance to the illusion.

Perhaps the most obvious power is that held by teachers and supervisors over undergraduate or more advanced professional trainees.

The graduate student, including the ABD (all-but-dissertation), continues to be in a powerless position until the degree is safe in hand. Even then, the residual power of former teachers that goes with writing letters of verification of training or letters of recommendation for the former students is not inconsiderable.

A young man who had been employed for several years in a professional capacity needed a letter of verification of training hours from his dissertation chairman. The professor had never come to terms with his rage at his former student who had refused to work on the professor's own project as his dissertation. The professor's main goal was to grind out another publication for himself (lest he perish!).

The former professor not only refused to write the letter but intimated that, if he did, the verification would not be forthcoming. The young man finally had to take the case to court, a form of formal power that can be viewed in this instance as analogous to one's parent's use of the power to protect the child from the abusive power of the other parent.

It is to the shame of some institutions that faculty members wield their power arbitrarily and sadistically, using their students as pawns in the power politics of the institution. But in one form or another, the abuse of power can be found in every segment of society.

Words

Most of us can probably recall the childhood chant:

*Sticks and stones can break my bones
But names will never hurt me.*

Although we may not have identified this ditty as a power tactic, we knew instinctively that it was. We knew we were in the power position when we told our adversary, "Your words are powerless. They cannot touch me. You are the one who is impotent." This stance is not unlike that of the abused child who says to himself, "You can kill me but you can't make me cry!"

A woman who had been terrorized throughout her childhood by her older brother, and whose parents did nothing to protect her, said "The only thing I could do to get my brother was with words and my tongue. He could hit and punch me. If I tried to hit him back he'd just laugh. All I could do back, the only equal power I had was to cut him down with my tongue. I had to use words as armor and weapons. But he did the ultimate. He stopped talking to me and never talked to me again. He took his jacks and went home because he couldn't compete."

But in the final analysis, she felt defeated by his silence. In effect he said, "You are powerless to get me to respond." He used silence as his weapon to counteract her words. What is sad is that they both have lost an important relationship. Winning the power struggle took precedence.

The person who has to have the last word is more interested in establishing power and control over the other than in having real communication, negotiation, or conflict resolution. The need for power drives out the possibility of intimacy.

Freeway Duels

Anyone who has been tailgated at speeds of 60 miles an hour or more on a crowded freeway knows what it is to have raw, naked, malevolent power breathing down one's neck. The sane solution is to move to another lane as soon as it is safe. The rageful solution is tempting but probably also suicidal: "Slam on the brakes and let him eat it!" As did the loser in similar square-offs in days of old on narrow plank sidewalks in the Old West, one steps off the sidewalk into the muddy gutter. And, quite probably, he or she will spend a good part of the day stewing over the humiliation of that loss. The odds are high that, before the day is over, the victim will exert his or her power over someone else in order to set the internal regulator of self-esteem back on an even keel.

Elitism

The American Heritage Dictionary defines the world "elite" as a "narrow and powerful clique." An attitude of elitism reflects a need for superiority, but also, primarily, for the power that is justified by that superiority.

First, the elitists declare themselves to be superior to others by virtue of some supposedly objective criterion. It may be a religious group that claims moral superiority which affords it the only key to the kingdom of God. It may be a social group in which the basis for claimed superiority is money. It may be a professional group in which the rationalization is participation in a specific training program. What marks the difference between a group that is organized around shared interests and goals, and the elitist group, is the latter's will to power.

The elitist group arrogates power to itself, justifying it by virtue of the self-proclaimed superiority. It then moves to widen its sphere of power beyond its own ranks, to gain more and more control. The drive for power and control is masked by stated values that serve to rationalize the group's ambition. The "narrow and powerful clique" may claim to have a dedication to the pursuit of excellence; but the driving force behind elitism is, ultimately, the quest for power and control.

Some who join do so in order to be able to participate in the power of the group, much as the infant participates in the power of the mother. Just as we see "guilt by association," we also see power or prestige by association. Some outside of the elitist group submit to its judgment unquestioningly, "buying into" the rationalization. Heads down, they accept their lot of being deemed "less than." They may both admire and envy the elite. Those who question or confront the power of the elite are met with contempt. Their protest can only be proof of their inferiority. Elitism is logically impenetrable.

It is only through recognition of the irrelevancy of the elite to one's own life, when a security based on intrinsic power and healthy self-esteem exists, that an individual can resist being hostage to the judgment of worth handed down by the "narrow and powerful clique." However, when this clique actually attains political power and is able to affect the individual financially or professionally or in some other significant way, the power issue per se may have to be joined. When the clique is able to affect one's life in reality, it is no longer irrelevant. However, the issue can only be effectively joined if others do not "buy into" the judgment of superiority on the part of the elitist group. We see this happening in South Africa where "white supremacy" and the power that has gone with it are being challenged. If power is not shared, and particularly if it is not benevolent, it is likely that it will be overthrown, whether within a family or within a nation.

Name-Dropping

Name-dropping is a power tactic associated with elitism. The name-dropper would like to be part of the powerful elite, and fantasies that he or she actually is by virtue of some little or peripheral contact with a person of power or status. The name-dropper implies that he or she is a crony or confidante of the well-known figure. There is a further implication that he or she has influence on this individual. It has been said that the illusion of power confers power itself, and sometimes name-dropping works in achieving the wish to be seen as part of the powerful elite.

Those who are overly impressed or intimidated by power, whatever its form or shape, readily make the inference wished by the name-dropper and relate to him as though *he* were a powerful figure himself. This, then, confers power upon him. The name-dropper has borrowed the power of the admired figure and has made it his own.

Rite of Passage

Every fall on college and university campuses, a drama of power and pride is re-enacted. Incoming students, eager to be accepted into prestigious sororities and fraternities, submit to what can be viewed as a rite of passage that has as its unconscious aim, the exorcism of childhood's powerlessness and admission to the ranks of the powerful parental figures.

The would-be members attend rushing parties in their best attire, on their best behavior, trying to win the approval of the group to which they seek admittance. Once chosen, as pledges they submit to domination and to public humiliation. Finally, in secret ceremonies, they are granted full membership.

In this allegory, childhood pressures to behave in a way aimed at avoidance of parental rejection, and avoidance of the humiliation brought about by relative powerlessness, are played out once again. But this time it is by choice, as though to master it, to say, "See, it's really all under my own control. I *choose* to let it happen." And finally, having taken control in this way, they are transformed into the powerful other; they are let in on the secrets of the grown-ups. Each year, the upperclassmen play out their identification with the aggressors in the role of quasi-parents who have the power to judge, to reject, and to humiliate. Through this identification they move to make the power of the parental figures their own.

Unfortunately, whatever gratification this drama may afford—to the degree that the identification with the powerful serves to cover over a deeply felt sense of powerlessness, to compensate for the shames of childhood, to provide an illusion of power within oneself—it will be shallow and temporary; it will have to be reenacted over and over lest the underlying feelings emerge and take over.

Negotiation

The scene is the automobile salesman's office. He and Tom Seymour are $75 apart on a $15,000 deal for a new station wagon. The salesman shakes his head and says he just can't do any better than $15,075. Tom gets up and thanks him for his time, saying he knows he can do better across town. He heads out the door and across the parking lot, not too fast, taking a last look at the demonstration model. Just as he is about to go out through the chain-link gate, the salesman comes running after him. "Wait! I just spoke to the boss and he gave me the O.K. for an even fifteen." A slight smile tugs at the corners of Tom's mouth. Game, set, match.

On his way home, the salesman swears at every car that gets in his way on the freeway, slams the front door of his house, and yells at his wife because dinner isn't ready.

The Religious Imperative

It is quite likely that a belief in some kind of God or gods is a universal phenomenon—not from person to person to be sure, but from culture to culture from the most primitive to the most sophisticated. One can hypothesize with respect to the implications of this; but which hypothesis is true, if any, is quite probably not verifiable.

From a theologian's viewpoint, this universality may stand as an indication of truth. From a psychologist's point of view, there are two possibilities readily at hand. The first derives from the inescapable truth that everyone begins life as an infant who is cared for by an adult, usually its mother—and usually, also, *primarily* its mother or a mother surrogate. If we think in terms of object relations development, recalling the infant's symbiotic oneness with the mother, and his or her participation in maternal omnipotence, we might speculate that this deep and intensely meaningful experience does not just disappear into the archaic unconscious. Indeed we do know that it comes into awareness with a longing for oneness, a longing that is sometimes, in adulthood, momentarily satisfied in the act of making love. Might not this archaic memory press for realization? That is, might it not press to be made real, as a lifelong avenue to the security felt by the nursing infant? And might that realization not take the form of a belief in something beyond the self that is characterized by the same omnipotence and oneness felt in symbiotic fusion with the nurturant object? Perhaps it is this felt imperative that becomes manifest in the certainty of a divine being.

From a more pragmatic point of view, but still within the psychological realm, the anxiety of contemplating a world operating with no central source of order or control, with no one tending the store, so to speak, may be too great to bear. If one cannot rely on a beneficent and all-powerful deity, one may be forced to depend even more upon powerful people to provide a semblance of order and control and the security this affords. This dependency upon people certainly has its down side, considering the corruptibility of power. God, one can assume, is beyond such corruptibility.

It is sad that certain ministers of God are not! The spectacle of the arrogance and greed of some religious leaders points the finger of truth to the words *power corrupts*. Instead of keeping to their designated role in the religious process, they borrow (or

steal) power from God and accept enormous amounts of attributed and financial power from their followers. All of this further
activates their own power needs. Power is heady stuff and the less
security there is in the intrinsic power of the self, the more corrupt-
ible is the spirit.

Capron (1984) writes:

The most important characteristic of the Eastern world
view—one could almost say the essence of it—is the awareness of the unity and mutual interrelation of all things and all
events, the experience of all phenomena in the world as manifestations of a basic oneness. All things are seen as interdepen-
dent and inseparable parts of this cosmic whole, as different
manifestations of the same ultimate reality. [p. 116]

If one can find meaning and purpose in being a well-
functioning and contributing part of something much larger than
the self, one's intrinsic and shared power as well as the self-
esteem associated with them will hopefully make the striving for
defensive and compensatory power unnecessary. Whether one is
a minister of God, or the president of a nation (Henry Brooks
Adams notwithstanding), or a teacher or a parent, power motives
will not obscure the vision of what has to be done to ensure the
smooth and peaceful and productive functioning of the whole.
This is true whether that whole is a family or a school, a nation or
the Family of Man. Although the likelihood of this world functioning in such a way is small, at least it can be a goal toward which
one can dedicate one's personal competence, one's will, and one's
healthy ability to act.

The Pervasiveness of Power

It would be reasonable to assume that each reader would be able
to think of still another "face of power." What one can see, by

way of such an exploration, is the fact that power is an inescapable fact of life. From the sublime to the ridiculous, from the evil to the banal, from the portentous to the insignificant, power issues are likely to play at least a contributing role in a large majority of situations or events.

If we listen or read attentively, we become aware of how the striving for power is taken for granted in our culture.

After the contentious interview of Vice-President George Bush by Columbia Broadcasting System's Dan Rather, a media critic noted that unfortunately the appearance of victory in combat becomes more important than clarity.

And on another T.V. channel a nutritionist said that it is not good to tell people what they must not eat, as they will then go out and eat it. "People with a healthy personality" she said, "don't like being told what to do!"

By and large, most of us are unaware of power's motivating impact. Some unseen navigator steers our ship on a course we have not consciously chosen. The more we become aware of power issues and are able to separate them from the problem at hand, the more constructive our choices are likely to be.

The psychotherapy patient who cannot accept anything good or useful from the therapist because this means placing oneself in a powerless and humiliated position, will feel good only if the therapist fails. The therapist's "failure" restores the patient's sense of power and pride. In this and other situations, there may be times when one has to lose an interpersonal power struggle in order to achieve an important goal. If our pride becomes the overriding issue, and if we lose sight of the larger issue we may end up an empty-handed winner.

Epilogue

How Is It with You?

If power issues can be identified, made explicit, and understood, in terms of both their defensive and their compensatory functions, power as an issue per se can be separated out from other factors such as wishes for love and nurturance. And only when power motives are depowered, only when they cease to run one's life, can one's creativity and achievement of life goals have a chance to be realized.

In this chapter I invite the reader to explore, from a power perspective, his or her problems in the worlds of work, love, play, and creativity. This is an exercise that can also be undertaken by a couple as a way to extricate their relationship from the dynamics of power-seeking. The possibility of true intimacy can surely be enhanced with the successful negotiation of this shared task.

Although it is beyond the scope of this book, an understanding of the power dimension of motivation and behavior within the individual might, hopefully, help people to have greater insight in choosing their leaders. Such understanding might also help leaders carry out their responsibilities more effectively, without interference from their personal will to power.

Your Family of Origin

It was within the context of the family into which you were born, and within which you evolved as a separate individual, that your inner psychological world was structured. Your relationship to power—to your own as well as to that of others—was also established there and then; and quite probably it is manifest in your here-and-now lives of work, love, play, and creativity.

Draw a diagram of that family, with everyone who played a significant role in it, including siblings and grandparents and any other integral member of the family system. Try to assess the distribution and balances of power, on the basis of the following questions:

- Who had it?
- Under what circumstances?
- How was it manifest?
- Did some have overt power while others had covert power?
- Was power used benevolently? How?
- Was power used malevolently? How?
- What was the nature of each person's self-esteem? How was it supported? Did it have to be protected?
- Who used power defensively?
- Who used power to compensate for underlying inadequacies?
- Were people related to on the basis of their own identities, or did some members of the family have to function as containers of power/powerlessness or pride/shame for other members? How did this come about? What behaviors were used to bring them about?
- What was the nature of each individual's intrinsic power? What was the quality of the *I am,* the *I can,* and the *I will* for each? What were their special talents? Were these appreciated or envied?
- Was envy a significant factor in the family dynamics? What were its effects on relationships? Who envied whom? Why? How did the envy manifest itself? Did some family members attempt to spoil others?
- What faces of power can you identify as characteristic of your family of origin?

Assessing Your Own Power

The "I am."   Do you have a secure sense of who you are, of your own boundaries, of a sense of self-sameness over time and changing circumstances? Do you feel connected with your innate intrinsic power, the abilities of your mind and body, and your own creative processes? Or do you feel yourself to be defined and limited by the needs of others? Have you distorted your sense of who you are in order to protect important others and your safe connection with them? Have you cut yourself off from your intrinsic power because of guilt or anxiety about having it and using it? Do you ever say, "I don't know who I am"? The amorphous self is a helpless and powerless self.

The "I can."   Somewhere between the illusory states of omnipotence and impotence lies the reality of competence. Both impotence and omnipotence are defensive forms of power and are not based on the reality of who a person is. The sense of mastery, competence, and effectiveness is central to intrinsic power. Do you maintain a stance of powerlessness as necessary to the role you play in the family system? Do you have to be the container of your mother's (or father's) inadequacy? Do you also have to be the container of either one's grandiosity? Do you need grandiosity yourself as an antidote to the shame and humiliation and anxiety that are the consequence of your defensive impotence? Do you have to be powerless because you are afraid of your aggression and the level of anger behind it? Do you make yourself harmless to those you care about?

The "I will."   Do you have a clear sense of your own intentionality? Is it expressed in positive ways as a statement about who you really are and what you want in your life? Or is it expressed negatively and reactively in the service of rage or despair because you are blocked in both the *I am* and the *I can?* Is your will oppositional in quality when its main function is to win the power struggle?

To whom do you attribute power in your life as a whole? Do you still experience yourself as a child in a world of grown-ups? Do you feel fully adult except when in the presence of your parents? Do you then revert to childhood patterns of relating to them? Do you carry attitudes toward your parents into your relationship with an intimate partner, feeling that you are in their power, being angry or frightened about how they might react to something you do? Are you unable to move beyond the protegé stance with regard to a mentor? What feelings does a mentor's attributed power stir up in you? Do you bring out childish ways of fighting parental power such as oppositionalism or rebellion? How does your readiness to attribute power interfere across the board with your interpersonal life as well as your performance in your work? Does fear of the judgment of critics deter you from expressing your creativity whether in writing, painting, or any other domain? Do you lose your sense of who you are and allow the "powerful" other to define you according to his or her needs?

Who attributes power to you? Are you comfortable when this happens, or do you dislike being identified with parental figures because of your own negative attitude toward them? Do you take advantage of the situation and use this power to make yourself feel stronger and to inflate your own self-esteem? Do you then have to keep the other in a powerless position? Are you afraid the person will hate you because you have power, will envy you and be destructive toward you? Do you put yourself down, as a way to counteract the discomfort of having power attributed to you? Do you purposely show your impotence and then feel terrible because you have shamed yourself? How do you go about remedying this state of affairs? Is there a constant disequilibrium in the power balance, with futile attempts to establish parity?

Do you envy the power of others? Do you have to denigrate them in order to reduce the envy? What is the effect of this on the relationship? What stands in the way of your having your own power, so that you continue to feel deprived and envious? How do you contribute to this situation? Do you blame others for what you, in effect, do to keep yourself powerless?

Are you afraid others will envy you? It is quite likely that if you envy, you will be afraid of being envied. There is a tendency to project one's own feelings and attitudes onto others, and then to assume they feel the same as you do. Since hatred usually accompanies envy, the fear is as much of the hatred as of the envy itself. Envy carries a wish to destroy or overthrow. It is not comfortable to think others feel this way toward you, and thus an attitude of anxiety and even some degree of paranoia may develop when the envious person projects that envy into others about him or her. Do you refuse your own power so others will not envy you?

Do you feel guilty about being powerful? Are you afraid you may hurt important others with your power? Is this because of buried angers and resentments, or because of a bubbling rage at having to be powerless yourself in the interpersonal system? Are you afraid you will use your power to hurt, rather than toward productive aims?

How is your self-esteem tied to power? Does the inhibition of your own power, and the failure and inadequacy this inhibition generates, lead to feelings of shame or humiliation? What do you do to repair your self-esteem? Do you become needy for recognition and acclaim, or for reassurance as to your being worthy in some way or other? Do you require others to repair your self-esteem for you in these ways? Do you compensate for it by seeking symbols of power such as money and prestige? Do you have to be a "big-shot" in your professional world? Do these compensatory forms of power help you, or are you aware of feelings of powerlessness and shame that lie just under the surface? Do you have secret or fantasy power that helps you counteract these feelings?

Do you use power as a defense? If you are afraid of being powerless, do you use power defensively, to make sure no one can get power over you? How do you do it? With whom? And under what circumstances? How does it affect the relationship?

Do you have formal power? If you do, how do you exercise it? Does it become perfused with personal needs for power? Do you find gratification in keeping subordinates in their place? Do you identify with the aggressor? Do you turn passive to active, doing to others what you felt was once done to you?

Has power become eroticized for you? Does it "turn you on"? How is it manifest—in actual sexual behavior or only in fantasy? Do you get into situations of actual danger, physical or mental, in pursuit of eroticized power? Or does this sort of power get played out in innocuous sex games such as spanking or wrestling? Are you troubled by it? How does it affect your relationships in general? Where did it originate? Do the power issues that are played out in sex get in the way of intimacy?

What do your faces of power look like? It is to be hoped that an honest and thorough evaluation of the place of power in your emotional life will enable you to disengage from counterproductive strivings for power, and to develop your own intrinsic power. It should also enable you to carry out the responsibilities of formal power positively. The resultant self-awareness is likely to encourage your use of whatever power you have toward the achievement of better relationships, more effective functioning in your work, and a freer capacity to play and create.

REFERENCES

Adler, A. (1930). Individual Psychology. In *Psychologies of 1930,* ed. C. Murchison. Worcester, Mass.: Clark University Press.

Bartlett, J. (1982). *Familiar Quotations.* 11th ed. Boston: Little, Brown and Co.

Bion, W. (1967). *Second Thoughts. Selected Papers on Psycho-Analysis.* New York: Basic Books.

Bjerre, A. (1927). *The Psychology of Murder.* New York: Da Capo Press, 1981.

Boszormenyi-Nagy, I., and Framo, N., eds. (1965). *Intensive Family Therapy.* New York: Hoeber.

Capron, F. (1984). *The Tao of Physics.* Revised. New York: Bantam.

Deutsch, M. (1960). The effect of motivational orientation upon trust and suspicion. *Human Relations* 13:122–139.

Erikson, E. (1950) *Childhood and Society.* New York: Norton.

Etchegoyen, R., Lopez, B., and Rabin, M.(1987). On envy and how to interpret it. *International Journal of Psycho-Analysis* 68:49–61.

Evans, Bergen. (1968). *Dictionary of Quotations.* New York: Delacorte.

Frank, J. (1987). The drive for power and the nuclear arms race. *American Psychologist* 42:337–344.

Freud, S. (1923). *The Ego and the Id. Standard Edition* 19:1–66.

———(1931). *Female Sexuality. Standard Edition* 21:223–243.

Guntrip, H. (1969). *Schizoid Phenomena, Object Relations and the Self.* New York: International Universities Press.

Haley, J. (1969). *The Power Tactics of Jesus Christ.* New York: Grossman.

Heider, J. (1985). *The Tao of Leadership.* Atlanta: Humanics Limited.

Horner, A. (1978). *Being and Loving.* New York: Jason Aronson.

———(1984). *Object Relations and the Developing Ego in Therapy.* 2nd ed). New York: Jason Aronson.

Lippitt, R., and White, R. (1958). An experimental study of leadership and group life. In *Readings in Social Psychology,* ed. G. E. Macoby, T. M. Newcomb, and E. L. Hartley, 3rd ed. New York: Holt.

Macdonald, J. (1986). *The Murderer and His Victim.* 2nd ed. Springfield, IL: Charles C. Thomas.

Mahler, M., Pine, F., and Bergman, A. (1975). *The Psychological Birth of the Human Infant.* New York: Basic Books.

Martin, J. (1988). *Who Am I This Time?* New York: Norton.

McDougall, J. (1987). In A. Wolfson, Toward the further understanding of homosexual women. *Journal of the American Psychoanalytic Association* 35:165–173.

Miller, A. (1968). *I Don't Need You Anymore.* New York: Bantam.

Nietzsche, F. (1963). The will to power. In *Reality, Man and Existence,* ed. H. J. Blockham, New York: Bantam.

Piaget, J. (1955). *The Child's Construction of Reality.* London: Routledge and Kegan Paul.

Racker, H. (1957). Contribution to the problem of psychopathological stratification. *International Journal of Psycho-analysis* 38:223–239.

Sagan, C. (1985). *Contact.* New York: Simon and Schuster.

Schafer, R. (1954). *Psychoanalytic Interpretation in Rorschach Testing.* New York: Grune and Stratton.

Shulman, M. (1987). On the problem of the id in psychoanalytic theory. *International Journal of Psycho-analysis* 68:161–174.

Slipp, S. (1984). *Object Relations: A Dynamic Bridge Between Individual and Family Treatment.* New York: Jason Aronson.

Sours, J. (1980). *Starving to Death in a Sea of Objects.* New York: Jason Aronson.

Stensrud, R. (1979). Personal power: a Taoist perspective. *Journal of Humanistic Psychology* 19:31–41.

Stoller, R. (1975). *Perversions.* New York: Pantheon.

Winnicott, D.W. (1965). *The Maturational Processes and the Facilitating Environment.* New York: International Universities Press.

———(1986). *Home Is Where We Start From: Essays by a Psychoanalyst.* New York: Norton.

———(1987). *Babies and Mothers.* Reading, MA.: Addison-Wesley.

Wolfson, A. (1987). Toward the further understanding of homosexual women. Panel Report. *Journal of the American Psychoanalytic Association* 35:165–173.

Yochelson, S., and Samenow, S. (1976). *The Criminal Personality.* Vols. I and II. New York: Jason Aronson.

INDEX